# HOW NOT TO GET SCREWED BY YOUR ATTORNEY

Also by Arthur Lyons

Non-fiction

*The Second Coming: Satanism in America*
*Satan Wants You: The Cult of Devil Worship in America*
*The Blue Sense: Psychic Detectives and Crime* (with Marcello Truzzi)

Fiction

*The Dead Are Discreet*
*All God's Children*
*The Killing Floor*
*Dead Ringer*
*Castles Burning*
*Hard Trade*
*At the Hands of Another*
*Three With a Bullet*
*Fast Fade*
*Unnatural Causes* (with Thomas T. Noguchi)
*Physical Evidence* (with Thomas T. Noguchi)
*Other People's Money*
*False Pretenses*

# HOW <u>NOT</u> TO GET SCREWED
# BY YOUR ATTORNEY

## WHAT YOU NEED TO KNOW
## TO PROTECT YOURSELF

Dudley Gray & Arthur Lyons

A Citadel Press Book
Published by Carol Publishing Group

A Citadel Press Book
Published by Carol Publishing Group
Citadel Press is a registered trademark of Carol Communications, Inc.

Editorial, sales and distribution, rights and permissions inquiries should be addressed to Carol Publishing Group, 120 Enterprise Avenue, Secaucus, N.J. 07094

In Canada: Canadian Manda Group, One Atlantic Avenue, Suite 105, Toronto, Ontario M6K 3E7

Carol Publishing Group books may be purchased in bulk at special discounts for sales promotion, fund-raising, or educational purposes. Special editions can be created to specifications.

Manufactured in the United States of America
10   9   8   7   6   5   4   3   2   1

Library of Congress Cataloging-in-Publication Data

Gray, Dudley,
    How not to get screwed by your attorney : what you need to know to protect yourself / Dudley Gray and Arthur Lyons.
        p.      cm.
    "A Citadel Press book."
    ISBN 0-8065-1778-6 (pbk.)
    1. Attorney and client—United States—Popular works.   I. Lyons, Arthur.   II. Title.
KF311.Z9G73   1996
340'.023'73—dc20
                                                            95-50272
                                                            CIP

*For my daughter, Cindy, who teaches the mentally impaired, my son Jeff, who defends the accused, and my son Dudley II, a judge who sits on the criminal bench, none of whom think about billable hours.*

—*Dudley Gray*

*For my wife, Barbara Lyons, the* true *love of my life. (This declaration herewith and hereby renders all other dedications null and void.)*

—*Arthur Lyons*

# Contents

## Appendixes

B:  Fee Agreement for Criminal Attorney             193
C:  Sample Legal Bill                               195
D:  Petition for Probate                            198
E:  Insurance Company Settlement Offer
    Agreement                                       200
F:  Petition for Marriage Dissolution               202
G:  Response to Petition for Dissolution            204
H:  Schedule of Assets for Dissolution              206

    Bibliography                                    211
    Index                                           213

# Acknowledgments

We would like to thank some good lawyers—the best of the breed—for their help on this book: David Baron, David Aleshire, Jeffrey Fromberg, and Elaine Hill.

# Introduction

Two tourists from Iowa are on a tour of Forest Lawn, the monumental Los Angeles cemetery, when one of them notices a headstone that reads: "Here lies Tom Brett, a good attorney and an honest man." The tourist turns to the tour guide and remarks, "You have peculiar burial practices in California."

"How's that?" asks the tour guide.

"You put two bodies in the same grave."

Everybody has heard at least one lawyer joke along similar lines. Why are these kinds of jokes, about a group of well-paid, high-status professionals, so popular? Probably because they have the ring of truth.

The American public distrusts lawyers. The reason is simple: Experience. Most of us, at one time or another, have found ourselves in need of a lawyer's services. And we've come away feeling like the victims of a mugging. As Fred Rodell, former professor of law at Yale University Law School, said some years ago, "It is pretty hard to find a group less concerned with serving society and more concerned with serving themselves than the lawyers."

The cold, hard fact is that the American middle class is being systematically ripped off by the legal profession. Not occasionally, not intermittently, but consistently and as a matter of practice. Consider this: Annually lawyers in this country are currently receiving 3.25 percent of the U.S. Gross Domestic Product, or $185.6 *billion*.

In California, which has one of the largest ratios of lawyers to population of the fifty states, the facts are even

more startling. The entire 1993 state budget, larger than that
of Canada or of the majority of ten other industrialized
nations, amounted to $52,185,000,000. By contrast, in that
same year, California lawyers collected $32 billion. With its
$52 billion, the state pays for education, health and welfare,
parks and recreation, police protection, prisons, highways,
infrastructure, a sophisticated water system, and a myriad of
other public services. California's 140,000 lawyers provide
none of the above services. In fact, in many cases, they add to
their cost.

So what exactly *do* lawyers produce for all that money?
When a cabinetmaker makes a table, he has produced
something tangible and durable on which you can set your
china. When an architect designs a building, the building is
there for posterity, or at least, one hopes, for a few years.
Lawyers produce words. Not truths, only words. Words that
are usually intentionally vague, overcomplicated, overly technical, and often meaningless when taken out of the limited
context in which they were written. As Will Rogers once
remarked, "The minute you read something you can't understand, you can almost be sure it was drawn up by a lawyer."

In other words, lawyers do not produce anything of any
lasting value—and they get paid extremely well for it. According to the American Bar Association, the average estimated
gross income per lawyer in this country is $232,000 a year.
Mind you, we said *average*. In a 1993 evaluation of the twenty
largest law firms in the United States, the *Wall Street Journal*
found that in 1992 the average partner in those firms made
$406,000 and that the average annual billings of the 16,000
lawyers comprising the twenty firms was $324,711.

How do they get away with it? That's easy. Because they
can. Not having any yardstick as to what legal services should
cost, clients are often reluctant to protest their lawyers' bills.
And that reluctance is often amplified by fears of alienating

the person representing them in matters that can spell economic or personal disaster.

This is not to say that all lawyers are crooks. Some *are*, but the majority are reasonably honest and hard-working (by their own definition of those terms), are respected members of their communities, do civic work, contribute generously to charities, and belong to the local Rotary and Lions clubs. The problem is that they *all* operate within a system of their own creation, in which the rules are skewed in their favor. A person can hire the most ethical attorney, one who plays strictly and meticulously by those rules, and can still end up getting screwed. In fact, it is *inevitable* because it is ingrained in the system. The government is supposed to frown on monopoly in business and has even made it illegal in many instances. But the government has endorsed—and actually *mandated*—monopoly in the legal system by decreeing that in order for one to become a player in the system, he must get a government-approved certificate saying that he has gone through law school and passed the bar exam. Once in possession of that certificate, the lawyer becomes part of a powerful elite which has total control of your legal affairs.

Your lawyer is a lawyer, the other side's lawyer is a lawyer, prosecutors are lawyers, judges are lawyers, and a huge percentage of state legislators and members of Congress are lawyers. Thus, lawyers make the laws, debate the finer, often unclear points of the laws they've made, and, finally, interpret the laws. It's like playing cards with four people who are working together. Your chances of coming out whole are greatly reduced.

Such absolute power is inevitably corrupting. Because lawyers are aware of their control over the system, they will charge whatever they feel like charging for whatever level of service they feel like providing. No one in his right mind would go into a used car dealership and say, "I have $20,000 to

buy an automobile. Tell me the best car for my needs, charge
me a fair price, and I'll take it home and be happy." Yet this
happens thousands of times a day in law offices across the
country.

When you make an appointment with an attorney, the
game is already stacked against you. You have a problem—
often a *big* problem that can have a major impact on your
life—and the lawyer knows this. Depending on the arrangement you make, the attorney will either charge you for how
much time he or she spends on your case, anywhere from $100
to $500 an hour, or a percentage of whatever settlement the
attorney ends up getting for you in court, usually between 30
and 50 percent, after expenses. In other words, the attorney
has set himself up as your partner, without assuming any of
your risk.

For this exorbitant sum of money, the attorney will
promise you nothing. If something goes wrong with your car
and you take it to a mechanic, you'd undoubtedly stop
payment on your check if you drove the car home and the
problem wasn't fixed. If you have an emotional problem and
pay a psychiatrist $100 an hour to talk about it, you may not
solve your problem, but at least you know you got your full
hour for your money (or at least fifty minutes). If you hire an
attorney, on the other hand, your problem may not get fixed
and you probably won't get all the professional time you'll get
billed for. The only thing you can be sure of is that you *will* pay
your legal fees. Otherwise, the attorney will sue you and you'll
just have to hire another attorney. Ignorance of the law will
never keep a losing lawyer from collecting his pound of flesh.

There are approximately 850,000 lawyers in the United
States, or one lawyer for every 312 people. And their ranks are
swelling. As society becomes more and more complex, the
need for deciphering that complexity grows. In the past
twenty years, the number of lawyers in America has doubled,
whereas the population has increased by 20 percent.

Not surprisingly, the number of lawsuits in this country has grown proportionally. More than twelve million lawsuits, or one per every twelve households, are filed in U.S. courts each year. Has the proliferation of lawyers been a response to the growing need for their services, or vice versa? Perhaps to some extent it cuts both ways. But there is no doubt lawyers don't just service their clients; they do their best to *create* clients.

It is not surprising that the lawyer-lawsuit boom began at the same time the ban was lifted on legal advertising by the U.S. Supreme Court. Overnight, professionalism fled the palace of justice and business took over. Lawyers were suddenly free to sell the public the myth that every social and individual problem has a legal solution, and they could raise public expectations and greed by pitching their wares like snake-oil salesmen. "Been hurt? Got a pain? Call 1–800–LAWYER. We'll get you big bucks...even if the accident was your fault!"

Another major force behind the current litigation explosion is the American Trial Lawyers Association (ATLA), a Washington, D.C., group which spends millions of dollars each year lobbying to thwart any federal legislation aimed at tort reform, the revamping of the civil justice system. ATLA members claim that their efforts protect the rights of every American seeking legal damages for an injury. Their claim to being caretakers of the public good, however, has been questioned by critics as a smokescreen for their real agenda, which is to fatten lawyers' wallets. During the debate on the 1991 Civil Rights Act, after ATLA managed to defeat an amendment by U.S. Senator Mitch McConnell of Kentucky which would have capped at 20 percent the amount of money lawyers could collect from their clients, McConnell remarked, "The plaintiffs' lawyers are interested in victims only insofar as that gives them a lawsuit. They are not interested in victims when it comes to distributing the proceeds from the lawsuit."

In 1993, at the annual ATLA convention in San Francisco, lawyers converged to get tips on advertising from a company specializing in "dignified law firm marketing" and to learn about "hot" new areas in tort law. But mostly they attended "litigation groups," where they picked up helpful hints about trying specific lawsuits. Some of these litigation groups are so specialized that they border on the bizarre, such as the automatic door opener group, the breast implant group, the bicycle manufacturers' group, the penile implant group, and the people-who-have-been-attacked-in-hotel-rooms group. There are around eighty such ATLA groups, thirty of which have been formed in the past two years, indicating that lawyers see such networking as a valuable tool in expanding the parameters of tort law and increasing jury awards for damages. ATLA recently changed its name to Consumer Lawyers of America.

Up until the early 1970s, except for perhaps being gouged by a probate or divorce attorney, the average person had little exposure to the legal profession. But with the advent of advertising, greed and hope were dished out over the airwaves as consumers were promised huge cash settlements for injuries or assumed that a lawyer could wave a magic wand and make their financial problems disappear. An already litigious society became more litigious. The answer to the viewing public's problems was to sue.

Fired from your job for incompetence? That doesn't matter. You can sue your employer for "unlawful termination." Your landlord tossed you out because you haven't paid rent in six months? Sue for abrogation of your civil rights. Your boss made a remark about your dress that you consider salacious? Sue for "sexual harassment." As the lawyers created more caselaw and expanded the public's perception of its need for lawyers, the number of lawyers mushroomed.

But while increased exposure logarithmically multiplied lawyers' profits, it also increased the public's disillusionment with the profession. Once involved with an attorney, the average person soon found out that nobody wins except the attorney. What he or she was sold in the way of expectations melted like a snowman in July. Television and newspaper reports announced huge judgments awarded in liability cases. What the stories didn't say, but what the litigants found out once they were involved, was that the plaintiffs would only get *thirty-seven cents of every dollar*. The other sixty-three would walk off in the attorneys' briefcases. The stories also didn't talk about the emotional pain and suffering such litigation brings to the participants, nor the incredibly long, frustrating, and economically draining process of getting a final judgment.

Interestingly, many lawyers themselves agree with the public's dim view of their profession. According to a 1991 study by the *Rutgers Law Review*, 60 percent of the attorneys surveyed admitted to personally knowing of instances of legal bill padding by themselves or their colleagues, and 17 percent admitted to having billed more than one client for the same work. Similarly, a 1994 survey conducted by the California State Bar and the Commission on the Future of the Legal Profession found that 63 percent of the lawyers questioned believe there are too many lawyers, while less than half believe that most of their fellow practitioners have "high ethical standards."

The disillusionment with the legal profession is not just limited to the general public or even legal consumers. A lot of lawyers *themselves* don't like what they do, with nearly one-third of the attorneys responding to the California survey saying that they wish they'd chosen another profession.

As the greed and arrogance rampant in the legal profession became exposed and glaring, the venerated lawyer of the 1950s became the villified thief of the 1980s and 1990s. At the same time, the law became the yuppie profession of choice, as the participants of the "Me First" generation saw it as the quickest way to get that BMW they had dreamed about since college.

This book was not written to lay out social remedies for restructuring the American legal system. We recognize that need, but it is beyond our scope. We wrote it to help guide you, the average citizen, through the shark-infested waters of the legal system.

The first part of the book deals with the common practices of attorneys, how they charge and what they charge for, and how they overbill and pad those charges to drive up the costs to their clients.

The second part deals with how to combat these practices and how to minimize the monetary damages you could suffer at the hands of your attorney. It will tell you how to avoid lawyers whenever possible (and advisable), how to sift through the baloney of advertising, how to pick an attorney who will represent you fairly and honestly, and how to determine if the attorney you picked is competent and honest.

The third part of the book takes up those stressful life problems—divorce, probate, real estate transactions, personal injury, bankruptcy, criminal prosecution—for which one might need to hire an attorney and how to contend with the "tricks of the trade" commonly employed by those legal specialists to get into your pocketbook.

Most people who hire an attorney for the first time do so blindly, not knowing what to expect. Once they have hired one, they often take a passive approach, partly out of dependence on the lawyer's skills to navigate the bewildering legal process and partly out of the feeling that it would be better to expend one's energies fighting the common enemy than to add another adversary to the fray by second-guessing one's own counsel. Passivity is just what lawyers count on when they hand their clients their bills. *To take a passive attitude toward your own case and to rely totally on your attorney to resolve your legal problems in a satisfactory way could be deadly not*

*only to your pocketbook, but also to the outcome of your case.*
We will attempt to show you in this book how you can keep
control of your attorney and his or her bills and at the same
time *improve* your chances of gaining the legal result you
want.

Although one of the authors is an attorney, we did not rely
solely on his expertise in putting this book together. We
interviewed dozens of attorneys specializing in various aspects of the law about their charges, their billing practices,
and their opinions on how to avoid getting stung when dealing
with lawyers. We found them to be surprisingly candid in
their answers and also in their realization that they are not a
loved group of people. "Everybody hates lawyers," one business attorney told us. "Even *lawyers* hate lawyers."

Some lawyers even extend that candor to their clients.
"When a client comes into my office, I tell him or her, 'If you
think you're going to get justice, forget it,'" said one attorney.
"'There is no such thing as justice. If I lose, you're going to say
I messed up, and if I win, I'm going to sock it to you and you're
going to say you got robbed.'"

Perhaps their candor was because they realized that the
game is so heavily stacked in their favor that the recourse of
the public is limited. We hope this book will do something to
change the odds, at least a little.

# PART I

## HOW LAWYERS STICK IT TO THEIR CLIENTS

# 1  Darwinism and Why Lawyers Think the Way They Do

Not all bears are exactly alike. Some are more playful than others, some are meaner, some lazier, some smarter, some more aggressive. But *all* bears are more like other bears than they are like anteaters. That is because they are programmed by a genetic code that has been shaped by evolution. So it is with lawyers.

Lawyers often tend to look a certain way, talk a certain way, discuss politics in a certain way, argue issues of the day a certain way. Just as a bear is the embodiment of "bear-ness," lawyers exude "lawyerliness." Before they apply to law school, all the while they are attending law school, and at the associate level when they are going through apprenticeships at whatever firm that has accepted them, these devotees of the law are subjected to powerful environmental forces which mold the way they act and think.

In the middle of the nineteenth century, Charles Darwin

revolutionized biology by publishing his theory of natural selection, a process resulting in the perpetuation of only those forms of life having certain favorable characteristics that enable them to best adapt to a specific environment. That principle of "survival of the fittest" is not only in operation in the biological world, but also in the legal world.

## Pre—Law School

### The First Cut: Who Applies

People who apply to law school exhibit certain common traits.

A disproportionate number are liberal arts or political science majors. They are usually intelligent, at least in an academic sense. Most of them score in the top percentiles of their class through high school and college. (Note, I am not using the term "intelligent" to mean they are especially well-rounded, possess an inordinate amount of common sense, or have a head for business. What I mean is that they take tests well, and thus usually excel academically.)

They usually possess a high degree of verbal skills, and the law is attractive to them because it is a field which requires the use of such skills.

They are argumentative and like to debate. They are also competitive, and when engaged in a verbal debate, like to win. Since such activity is the mainstay of the legal profession, going to law school is appealing.

They enjoy problem-solving and have a love of order and procedure. Since the law is basically a framework of regulations and decisions defining the structure of a society, the legal profession is a vocation that holds a strong attraction for such personality types. Few anarchists apply to law school.

They also smell money. Few jobs in the marketplace can offer the prospect of such high pay at the entry level. Many prospective law students view the law as the way to wealth and social prestige.

## The Second Cut: The LSAT

To get into law school, a student must take an exam called the Law School Aptitude Test, or LSAT, which allegedly is designed to identify those best suited for practicing law, and conversely, by implication, to weed out those who are not. In reality, the LSAT does neither.

For one thing, the format of the LSAT has been changed since the 1960s, basically to encourage more students to apply to law school. Spatial and mathematical problems have been eliminated along with questions that test general educational background. The number of logical-analytical questions was also reduced, leaving the primary focus of the test on verbal skills. According to law professor Mary Anne Glendon, "We have a situation where a test which makes no pretense of identifying talents relevant to the practice of law plays a significant role, along with college grades, in determining the ultimate composition of the country's lawyer population."

In other words, the natural selection process of law school favors survival for those students adept at verbal acrobatics, but who may possess little actual creative problem-solving ability and few mathematical skills.

Also, the LSAT is alleged by its promoters to test knowledge and skills which can't be improved by last-minute cramming. But there are quite a few companies making a lucrative living selling prep courses to students willing to pay. If such courses were worthless, it would seem that the word would have gotten around by now.

Once a student takes the LSAT, his score is tallied and he is notified what "percentile" he is in. This percentile represents, according to Brigham Young University law professor James D. Gordon III, "the inverse percentage chance you have of spending your life doing something honest."

## Law School: What It Teaches and What It Doesn't

### The Adversarial Frame of Mind

From the first day of the first class in law school, the student is trained to be combative. This is done by teaching through the Socratic method, whereby the professor never answers a question, except with another question.

A case is introduced in class by the professor, who then asks for arguments pro and con, explaining that there are always two sides to every argument and every point of law. If your argument favors a certain point of view, the professor will then ask other students to argue the other side of the issue. This is called instilling an "adversarial frame of mind," a battlefield environment in which conflict and argument are the arbiters of events. Halfway into his argument, a student may even be (and often is) ordered by the law professor to switch sides in the debate and defend the opposing side's point of view. This practice is supposed to train students for future law practice, in which they may be called upon to argue effectively for whichever side is paying them by the hour.

This is a far cry from what students were being taught in law schools fifty years ago, when emphasis was given to *avoiding* conflict rather than to initiating it. The emphasis in many law schools was instructing would-be lawyers how to find the common ground between arguments, mediate, work out problems, and avoid litigation. Moreover, not only does this method of teaching inculcate in students the belief that combat is the only answer, it also sends the message that there is no real truth in any legal argument, but only winning and losing—therefore it makes no difference which side one takes, as long as one is paid for it. If a nonlawyer acted that way, he'd be called a hypocrite, but in the profession of law, equivocal morality is extolled.

The sad fact is, the role that is promoted and venerated in law school is not that of the peacemaker, but of the litigator—

the student who gets up in front of the class and argues the most vehemently and persuasively, regardless of the content of his argument. And that hero-worship of the fighter is reflected in the general public's view of lawyers. In a 1993 poll of what lawyers people admired most, F. Lee Bailey and Perry Mason scored highest. It didn't seem to matter to respondents that Perry Mason existed only in Erle Stanley Gardner novels, only that he was a "winner."

### How to Think in Legalese

One significant trait which sets lawyers apart from nonlawyers is their use of the English language. They initially learn how different they will become in a first-year law course called "Legal Research and Writing."

For example, they learn to use words in pairs, such as "null and void" and "cease and desist." Some say this practice originated in English law when lawyers had two languages—Celtic and Anglo-Saxon—to choose from. Whether or not that is true, it is true that much legal writing is redundant and often downright confusing to a layperson.

The problem is that lawyers, in their zeal to write precisely, often overwrite to the point that the meaning of what they are writing becomes unclear, lost in a morass of adjectives, adverbs, and double negatives. "The Supreme Court has refined this art," says James D. Gordon III, "writing the world's only quadruple negative: 'This is not to say, however, that the prima facie case may not be met by evidence supporting a finding that a lesser degree of segregated schooling in the core city area would not have resulted even if the board had not acted as it did.' Government cryptographers have tried to decipher this sentence for years."

According to David Aleshire, a lawyer with the prestigious Orange County, California, firm of Rutan and Tucker, "In law school, you read nothing but cases in which people write like that, so you just do it. You just unconsciously start to pick up that way of using language. One time, I had an English teacher take a contract I'd written and cross out all the unnecessary words. It was a shock to see how much language I didn't need."

This use of legalese is reinforced when the fledgling lawyer goes to work for a law firm and is handed agreements drawn up by other lawyers to use as templates when drawing up his own agreements. The process is self-perpetuating, and soon the lawyer is incapable of thinking in nonlawyer language. It also breeds in the lawyer a feeling of superiority, of being smarter than the rest of the population (his or her future clients) because of the dubious distinction of being able to decipher legal babble. The only problem is that another lawyer might interpret the same legal babble in a completely different way.

### The Litigator versus the Planner

A major part of the law school bias toward litigation comes from the fact that law students are taught by arguing *case law*. A case by definition is a fight, an example of a situation in which something went disastrously wrong. If the conflict Smith had with Jones had been solved to their mutual satisfaction outside of the courtroom, *Smith v. Jones* would not have made it into the lawbooks. Students, therefore, are being educated in a world in which war is the norm and peace is an aberration.

Law professors don't teach their students how cases like *Smith v. Jones* could have been avoided through a process of compromise and negotiation, how such compromise and negotiation might have led to a more satisfying result for the warring parties, or how to isolate the crux of Smith and Jones's problem and help them solve it. The fact is, *90 percent of all lawsuits filed end up being settled out of court*. Unfortunately, most of them are settled only after clients on both sides have spent considerable sums of money and grief. What law schools should teach is how to short-circuit conflict and solve the problem before it goes to full-blown litigation. But, of course, the image of the problem solver and mediator is less glamorous than that of Perry Mason.

The current emphasis in law schools of looking at cases decided after rational discussion broke down fosters an inclination in students to see such scenarios as the norm. It makes them believe that such terrible occurrences are common in the everyday world from which they have been sequestered for three years. Therefore, when they get out of law school, they examine every contract for worst-case scenarios, no matter how far-fetched they may be or rare in real life. Lawyers are ill-prepared for planning to *avoid* a lawsuit or for drafting a document that will present not a problem but an acceptable solution.

Which would you rather have, an accountant who informs you before you file your income tax return that the deduction you are claiming is not valid under the law, or one who fills out your forms without comment, resulting in an IRS audit?

## Putting the Client's Interests First

This philosophy, currently popular in law schools and with the general public, goes hand in hand with litigation and conflict. Lawyers today are taught to advocate their client's position regardless of what that position may be. The lawyer is viewed as a "gun for hire," a mercenary who will fight for whichever side is paying him. The role of peacemaker and facilitator is thus minimized. Putting the client's interests first may sound admirable, and that is the way it is meant to sound. What that actually means, however, is open to interpretation.

Mary Anne Glendon sees the popularity of this principle among lawyers as actually self-serving in that it allows them to "look good while following the course of least resistance." Life becomes less complicated. A lawyer no longer has to worry about moral and professional obligations. Only what the client wants matters. If the client says, "We fight," the lawyer fights. But is a lawyer putting his client's interests first if the client is so emotionally caught up in his case that he exhorts the lawyer to carry it to a bitter conclusion, even if that conclusion will be ruinous to the client himself?

The most valuable traits a good lawyer can have is an analytical ability to isolate the crux of a problem, a feeling for common ground and consensus, the ability to anticipate future possibilities and make provision for them, and a thorough knowledge of the law. Unfortunately, these are traits law schools don't teach.

### The Intimidation Factor

In law school, students live in terror of their professors. The fear of being called upon and not knowing the answer to a question makes every law student break out into sweat. Students at a loss for words are regularly embarrassed and chastised in class. This breeds in lawyers an unwillingness to admit they don't know something and a reluctance to confess they were wrong. It also teaches them firsthand about the arts of intimidation and confrontation.

Lawyers generally like to use intimidation not only against other lawyers, but also against their own clients, to get them to bow to their advice and, later, to pay whatever they suggest. Lawyers emerge from law school with a feeling of superiority (a feeling they probably had before law school) due to having survived the three-year ordeal of work, anxiety, and professorial terrorism. They are chafing at the bit to give some of that terrorism back to the system and their clients. *They* are the professors now.

## Post–Law School

Once the fledgling lawyer has been tossed out of the nest, he or she is subjected to the forces of natural selection in the real world. If a young lawyer wishes to survive in the legal profession, certain personality traits will greatly enhance the chances of success. One such trait is rapaciousness.

A few years ago, a student who had passed the bar and been accepted by a law firm would undergo an apprenticeship during which he would be patiently trained and taught the reality of the world of law that he never learned in law school. During this period of time, he or she would work at a low salary, and firms didn't count on turning a profit on the novice for his or her first few years at the firm.

In the 1980s, competition among law firms became fierce, and firm-raiding became a not infrequent occurrence. This generated a situation in which the large firms were forced to go to bid for the best and brightest law school graduates.

Law schools, to some degree, have always participated in this process. Because it is important for the schools to place their graduates in high places, thereby enabling them to attract endowments and publicize the accomplishments of their alumni, they have always made available to recruiters from major law firms information about the students such as class standing, law review status, and membership in various legal student organizations.

As a result of cutthroat competition between firms, salaries offered law school graduates have skyrocketed in the past ten years, to the point that in the late 1980s and early 1990s, the beginning average salary for a law school graduate hired by a large firm reached $85,000. The result of the intensified competition for the best and brightest has had several results, one of them being that a primary trait law firm recruiters now look for in a prospective lawyer is *greed*. How many hours is he willing to work? What kind of debts does he have?

The new policy at large law firms is to hire go-getters, hungry, aggressive types who will not just handle business that comes to the firm, but will go out and recruit business for the firm. The term bandied about in law circles to describe the new system is aptly called "eat what you kill."

Those young attorneys who interview for positions at major law firms are commonly screened not for their legal acumen, but for their personality types. The big firms' partners want those young lawyers who are rapacious, who will bring in large profits for the firm—that is for them. The November 1992 issue of the *National Jurist*, a magazine for law students, surveyed major law firms to determine what qualities they were seeking in prospective associates. The answer came back: Someone who could "hit the ground running;" in other words, someone who could immediately generate billable hours and whom the firm did not have to spend a lot of time training. Samuel Hoar of Goodwin, Proctor unabashedly admitted that his firm favored applicants who had taken on summer work and part-time jobs because that "indicates that they are greedy and eager."

Up until the yuppified 1980s, the discussion of money or salaries was frowned upon during interviews of prospective associates, but during that decade such discussions became quite common. Students want to know how much they can make immediately so they can start paying off those student loans that got them through law school, and the partners are looking for those hungry students who will be able immediately to produce billable hours for the firm.

This natural selection process weeds out those students who look on the law as an honored profession, an art, and favors the survival of those contentious, litigation-prone Rottweilers who see conflict as a way to generate billable hours and who look upon preventive lawyering, i.e., the settlement of disputes outside the courtroom and the discouraging of litigation, as counterproductive to their interests. The peacemaker who tells the client he might be better off *not* suing is going the way of the mastodon; the greedy go-getter who has his eye on that new Mercedes, who is willing to go along with whatever his client wishes, even if it will be counterproductive to the client's interests, who is willing to even *inflame* those wishes by promising a big courtroom win, is propagating.

Because of all this, the old tutelage-apprenticeship system at many large firms has been scrapped, or at least severely hamstrung; firms aren't about to coddle some novice who's pulling down close to six figures a year. Consequently, young graduates have often been forced to learn as they go, a rude awakening for many who find themselves ill-prepared by law school for the everyday practice of law.

What they are taught by their mentors is that their time equals money, that an hour does not necessarily mean sixty minutes, and that the interests of the firm come before any personal agenda, or even before the interests of the client. The novice may not get much instruction about the practicalities of law upon joining the firm, but he will certainly and immediately be taught all about how to create cash flow for the firm.

Attorney-businessman Mark McCormack sums up the attitude of law school graduates in his Axiom of Delayed Rewards: "People who have sacrificed large amounts of time and money to get a professional credential—doctors, lawyers, MBAs—come away ferociously determined to get their investment back with interest—from the system and from you!"

# 2 Billable Hours

Lawyers charge for their services in different ways, depending on their inclination and the nature of the case.

One way is the *flat fee*. This is a fixed amount set by the individual lawyer for a specific service, such as handling a bankruptcy, filing an uncontested divorce, attending to certain tax matters, or drawing up papers of incorporation. These kinds of cases usually involve simply filling in the blanks on standard legal forms and take up very little of the attorney's time. In fact, often the paperwork is handled by a paralegal or even a secretary who works in the attorney's office and is only checked over by the attorney. The attorney can calculate his costs to the penny and safely tack on a sizable profit.

Another method of charging is the *contingency fee*. Contingency fees are common in personal injury cases or other civil litigation in which the plaintiff is suing for major damages. The lawyer agrees to take on the client's case for a percentage of the eventual settlement. If the client is awarded nothing, the attorney gets nothing. Or so the theory goes. But theory and fact can be two different animals, as we shall see in a later chapter.

Although it has been effectively argued that the contingency system and some of the outrageous monetary awards it has spawned has had a disastrous effect on the cost of doing business in this country, and despite the fact that it often works more to the advantage of the attorney than the client, in certain instances hiring a lawyer on a contingency can make sense.

A third, and most common, way attorneys bill is *by the hour*. The hourly fee will depend on many things—the lawyer's reputation, his abilities, his office address—but in the long run boils down to what he or she can get away with. When charging by the hour, the attorney will usually exact a sizable retainer in advance and use it up as his hours on the case mount.

If you ever received a bill for an attorney's time, you probably had the nagging—perhaps screaming—feeling you were being grossly overcharged. You can rest assured that you are not paranoid and that your suspicions were probably justified.

Overcharging for legal fees is so ingrained in the system that it has become for many an accepted practice. Indeed, at many large firms it has become a *requirement*. In addition to salaries, large law firms typically spend considerable amounts of money for office space in high-rent office buildings and auxiliary expenses like plush office furnishings and fixtures to impress clients. Someone has to pick up the tab for all that overhead. Guess who? The clients they are seeking to impress.

One of the first lessons a fledgling attorney learns after leaving the law school nest is how to stick it to the client to preserve the firm's profit margin. And the corollary of that lesson is that if the attorney does not want to stick it to his client, he will be sticking it to himself.

The indoctrination process might go something like this:

After the novice—let's call him Phil—passes the bar exam and is accepted by a law firm of his choice, he is introduced by a managing partner to a senior associate—Stan—who will act as his supervisor and explain to him the "facts of life" that rule the new world which he is entering.

After being taken to lunch and given a tour of the firm's offices, Phil is ushered into Stan's office and offered a cushy chair. Stan takes his place behind his desk and begins the lecture.

"Congratulations, Phil, you're now a junior associate with Philbean, Philbean, and Smith. Your starting salary is $95,000 a year, and for that you'll be expected to work a minimum of forty hours a week, accent on the word 'minimum.' During your first year, you will bill clients at a rate of $100 per hour, and you'll be expected to generate $300,000 a year for the firm. After the first year, your billing rate will go up to $150 an hour."

At this point, Phil, who is no mathematical wizard, but possesses some arithmetic skills, looks a bit confused.

Stan, being perceptive, as all good attorneys must be, notices the hesitancy in his pupil. "Something bothering you?"

"It's just that forty hours a week at $100 per hour adds up to $200,000, not $300,000," Phil responds reluctantly. "Where does the other $100,000 come from?"

His mentor leans back and smiles amiably. "I had the same question when I joined the firm five years ago. It's all in your billable hours, which I'll explain in a minute. But first you have to understand the structure of the firm.

"You're a junior associate and get paid a salary, as I said. If all goes well, it won't take long before you're made an associate, which will entitle you to a small bonus at the end of the year. Next step up is senior associate, with a larger bonus, then junior partner, and finally, senior partner. Juniors get a share of the profits, but by far the largest piece of the pie goes to the seniors. Nobody but the seniors knows how the profits are divided and nobody will ever know until he or she attains entrance to that inner circle."

Stan's smile disappears and his manner becomes more serious. "If you don't become a full associate in eighteen months, my advice is to start looking for another job, because your chances for promotion will be dim. The same thing if you're not a senior associate within three to five years. And five years after that, if you haven't been tapped on the shoulder and asked to have lunch in the firm's dining room, you'll probably never become a partner. Some attorneys at the firm have been senior associates here for twenty years. They're the drones of the hive, secure in their positions as long as they make a profit for the firm, but resigned to the fact that that's all they'll ever be."

Phil, who never took Gouging 101 in law school, is still a bit foggy on the concept. But his *real* education is about to begin.

"Billable hours," Stan goes on, "that's what it's all about. How many dollars you can squeeze from every file. The trick is how to make forty minutes equal an hour, and it's not all that difficult.

"First, there are telephone calls. You won't be seeing many clients your first year, only witnesses, but you will have to call for interviews, interrogatories, and information. You will mostly be talking to bookkeepers, accountants, record keepers—underlings of our clients. No matter. A phone call is time, and time is money.

"The minimum time we bill for a phone call is one-fifth of an hour, or twelve minutes. It doesn't matter how short the call is; in fact, the shorter the better. That way, you can make more phone calls an hour and rack up your billing time. Also, if you talk thirty minutes or more, the person you're talking to could be keeping time records. Any questions so far?"

Phil, who has looked around Stan's plush office and wants one of his own, shakes his head.

Stan resumes his lecture. "One of the best ways to build up your hours is to review the file. Review the complaint, the answer, the depositions, the interrogatories, the documents, the legal briefs, the motions—review it all. Now, review doesn't have to mean sitting down and actually *reading* the file. If you *think about the case* when you are driving to work or going home—even when you are taking a shower—you are reviewing the case, so bill for it. You spend two hours a day driving to and from work; think about the case and don't forget to record the time."

"I think I'm beginning to understand," Phil says, smiling widely.

"Good," Stan replies, pleased at the progress of his pupil. "Another important tip: Get to know your opposition. He is not your enemy. On the contrary. He's probably a junior associate, just like you, and is trying to get ahead. You can get ahead together. Take him to lunch and discuss the information you need. He'll appreciate it. He has billable hours and so do you.

"This courtesy shouldn't just be extended to your adversary. If you have a question, don't hesitate to get in touch with one of your colleagues at the firm and ask his opinion. Back this up in your file by inserting a memo that says, for example, 'I would appreciate the comments of the Real Property Division before proceeding further.' That will give you backup in case the client questions the bill. The document will be read and initialed by half a dozen lawyers in the firm, each taking about five minutes and simultaneously charging half an hour for 'review and giving an opinion.' This spreading of the wealth will ingratiate you with your colleagues and let them know you're a team player."

Stan opens his desk drawer and takes out four legal folders. He hands them across the desk to Phil. "This will be your first assignment. They are all product liability actions. Two are against ladder manufacturers, one against a shower door company, and one against a general building contractor."

Phil glances at the files while Stan drones on. "Demurrers have been filed in three of the cases. You need to prepare a demurrer to the fourth. Go through the other files and you will find the paperwork similar. Use that for reference. Use the same points and authorities, but those documents are thirty pages long each, and remember, you don't grind out thirty pages of a highly complex document in an hour. You can obviously copy them in a short period of time, but remember, you are a professional, and you must review each page, which should work out to, say, thirty minutes a page. Just because one client has the same problem as the others and you can use the same paperwork doesn't mean he gets a free ride. Any questions?"

Phil glances at his watch. "Do I charge the client for this time we spent talking about his case?"

"Absolutely," Stan says, beaming, proud of his newest pupil. "Welcome to the firm."

All this may sound unethical, if not downright illegal, but the cold, hard fact is that much of it is standard practice at major law firms.

Most law firms like Phil's have billing standards for various activities. A telephone call by or to an attorney, no matter how short, will be billed to the client at a minimum standard period of time—twelve, fifteen, or however many minutes specified by the firm. Firms have even been known to bill clients for telephone conversations even if the attorney never got hold of the client.

If a client goes beyond the standard time allotted, the next highest increment will be billed. For instance, if the firm's incremental time is one-fifth of an hour, or twelve minutes, and the conversation takes thirteen minutes, the client will be billed for twenty-four minutes. In other words, the client will be billed for more time than he talked.

If the minimum cost of a phone call is twelve minutes, the cost of dictating a letter would naturally be more, perhaps fifteen minutes, even though a one-paragraph letter might be rattled off in a minute and a half.

Let's say the lawyer arrives at the office at eight and starts making telephone calls, preferably ones he knows will be of short duration. He might call lawyers he knows are not in until nine. A secretary answers, confirming Lawyer X will not arrive until later, so he leaves a message to call back. Charge: $.2 \times \$200 = \$40$. The same thing happens when he calls Lawyer Y, except he gets a paralegal. He asks for, and receives, the courtesy of getting a ten-day extension to file an answer to a summons and complaint. He picks up the handset of his dictating machine and dictates a boilerplate letter confirming the agreement and the conversation. Time consumed: five minutes.

A secretary will later translate the message to formal language, ending with the standard, "Thank you very much for your courteous cooperation." Time logged: thirty minutes.

If by some chance Lawyer Y happens to be in his office, the two discuss the same subject and agree to the same extension. Of course, Lawyer Y will then dictate an almost identical confirmation letter and bill *his* client for the same thirty minutes. Thus, two clients have paid for one hour of time which consumed less than ten minutes.

If the client complains, he will be turned over to the credit manager, commonly dubbed the "account administrator," who will sit down with the disgruntled customer and go over the bill—all of which will be carefully documented—and decipher the cryptic entries, pointing out in detail when the work was done and who did it, and at the same time giving a rousing sales pitch about the brilliance of the firm's staff and how the client would be paying one hell of a lot more if he hired the firm's competitors. In most cases, the client will go away still thinking he's been overcharged, but feeling too dazed and helpless to do anything about it. If he continues to complain and complain loud enough, however, the bill might be submitted to the firm's partners for review and possible adjustment. Or the client might just be told to pay the full amount or face legal recourse.

In one of the most egregious instances of racking up billable hours, James E. Spiotto, a top partner at the prestigious Chicago law firm of Chapman and Cutler, billed clients $2,336,784 for 6,022 hours of work in 1993. That comes out to 16.5 hours a day, seven days a week, *every day of the year*. The 1993 total was up from the previous three years, during which he only racked up 5,000 hours a year, even though billings of even 3,000 hours are extremely rare. Although Mr. Spiotto's billing rate was $350 an hour, 2,336,784 divided by 6,022 equals $388. One would have to assume the other $38 an hour was billed for "expenses."

Ironically, the Spiotto affair came to light as a result of internecine warfare, after another Chapman and Cutler attorney, Maureen Fairchild, allegedly complained about Spiotto's billing practices. But the complaints backfired when it was revealed that Mrs. Fairchild had inflated her own bills to the tune of $275,000. The overbilling was done on a case that had been referred to Mrs. Fairchild by her husband, Gary Fairchild, a top attorney with another prestigious Chicago firm, the 455-attorney Winston and Strawn. Gary Fairchild later resigned from the law firm after allegations that he had improperly steered business to his wife and that he had misappropriated $500,000 of the firm's funds by falsifying expense reports and abusing his authority to approve payments.

Billing clients on the basis of padded time sheets is technically a form of fraud, prosecutable as "theft by deception," and an attorney who knowingly engages in such practices is subject to disbarment and civil litigation. Furthermore, partners of the offending attorney who shared in the firm's profits generated from the attorney's overbilling are also culpable in civil cases. The fact is, however, that such actions are rarely taken, usually only when the attorney infractions are so outrageous that they cannot be ignored. One reason is that the attorneys bringing the fraud action are probably doing the same thing to each other and passing on the overcharges to their clients.

In the mid-1970s, one of the authors (D.G.) learned that fact the hard way when hired by a group of investors interested in negotiating an operating agreement to manage the Ontario, California, Motor Speedway.

During the negotiations, I was notified by the attorney who had acted as bond counsel to the nonprofit corporation which had issued the bonds to finance the Speedway that in order to make the transaction legal, it would be necessary to amend the bond indenture.

Bonds, such as those issued for the Speedway, are merely a series of promissory notes bearing interest rates and terms of repayment. An indenture is a multi-paged document used to collateralize the bonds and give the bonds a security interest in the land and buildings. It is nothing more than the deed of trust or mortgage commonly used to borrow money to purchase a house. The indenture differs primarily in size and complexity, being a hundred or more pages of legal jargon spelling out the rights and duties of the bond holders and procedures in case of a default.

Although I could see no need to change the indenture, as all the bonds had already been sold and all that was to happen was a personnel change to manage the facility, the bond counsel disagreed, insisting changes be made. Unfortunately, I agreed to hire the distinguished lawyer's firm to do that.

After drafting the amendment—eight double-spaced

pages consisting of resumés of the proposed management group and a description of the amount of money to be invested—I mailed the document off to the law firm. A few days later I went to the firm's plush, high-rise office.

In a conference room, the bond counsel and an associate attorney discussed with me the amendment to the indenture. I found that they had rewritten the resumes of the principals to say exactly what I had, except in their own words. They had also revised the simple and understandable terms of the operating agreement into convoluted legalese, with a dizzying amount of cross-paged references, making it difficult for even other attorneys to understand. I was informed that this document was only a *first* draft, foretelling more legalese to come. Then I was invited to lunch.

In the firm's dining room, we were joined by four other attorneys and served a multicourse lunch, during which I was questioned enthusiastically about my experiences in the field of criminal law. These lawyers were all business attorneys. Few of them had ever seen the inside of a courtroom, never mind tried a criminal case, and they expressed interest in hearing about my most interesting cases. As I enjoyed telling "war stories" about my courtroom victories, I expounded on my exploits for thirty minutes to the fascinated audience. After lunch, I was asked some casual questions about the Speedway. I departed when the attorneys all brought out their yellow legal tablets and announced they had "other matters to discuss."

Thirty days later, the eight-page amendment to the indenture arrived in final form, along with a bill for $80,000 for attorney fees—$10,000 a page. That was a hell of a lot of money in those days.

After demanding a detailed statement of expenses, I received an itemized bill on which was included an hour-and-a-half in-house conference with six lawyers at a charge of $200 for each of the associates and $300 for the bond counsel—the "war story" lunch.

Fortunately, one of the investors, a wealthy car dealer, angrily confronted the distinguished bond counsel and settled for one-fourth of the amount billed, still far too much money for eight pages that never needed to be rewritten. But I have no doubts that the law firm made up the shortfall by billing six other clients for the same lunch—the "other matters" which were discussed after my departure.

There is an insider's joke lawyers tell. A lawyer dies and goes to heaven, where he is met by Saint Peter, who tells him he is being specially honored at his admission because of his age, being the oldest person to enter heaven since Methuselah. The lawyer, perplexed, says there must be some mistake in their records, that he is only fifty-five.

"There is no mistake," Saint Peter assures him. "You practiced law for thirty years. We have reviewed your records and according to your billable hours, you're nearly three hundred years old."

# 3   Just the Fax, Ma'am, Nothing But the Fax

Abraham Lincoln is credited with having once said, "A lawyer's time is his stock in trade." One hundred and fifty years later, that old adage holds true, except that thanks to the computer age and modern technology, there is a lot more stock in trade.

In Lincoln's day, a lawyer had to travel by horse and buggy to get to the courthouse. In today's supersonic age, distances between clients and courthouses have become moot. A trip that in Honest Abe's day would have taken six months can now be made in six hours. A lawyer from Washington, D.C., can represent a client in Los Angeles and love every minute of it. This is because of the Attorney Theory of Relativity, which says that time and space become warped at jet speeds, a fact every out-of-town client learns when he receives his bill for legal services.

The main principle behind the theory is that when travel

is involved, every attorney-hour becomes two and every five hours seven. How does that happen? Simple. Because of his reputation as a "big gun," New York attorney Goniff is hired by Client A to fly to San Francisco to handle his lawsuit. Client A is not only paying for the flight—first class, of course—but also for Goniff's travel time. But Client "A" is not Mr. Goniff's only customer, and Goniff has brought with him a file relating to the case of Client B. During the trip, while sipping martinis, Goniff goes over Client B's papers. Goniff has now doubled his billable hours—five to Client A and five to Client B. When he arrives at the airport, he then has to collect his baggage, find ground transportation, and settle in at his hotel, a minimum of an hour, more probably, two, to be tacked on to Client A's bill. Thus, five hours have become seven. Client B will be billed only for the five hours of flight time, unless, of course, Goniff was thinking about Client B's problems en route to the hotel from the airport.

But an attorney doesn't need to bill two clients for the same hour to double-bill. During litigation, the principal attorney frequently takes along an associate attorney to assist him during the trial. Sometimes an associate is needed to provide input or to question witnesses, but frequently he or she is there just to shuffle papers and provide a warm, costly body that gets billed to the client. Even though they may travel in the same car to the courthouse, the travel time is, of course, doubled.

A lawyer can also pad a client's bill by the *way* he or she charges. A lawyer may work on a case for three hours while on a plane, but bill the client for eight, using the rationale that he would have put in and been paid for a full eight-hour day if he had been in his office. It is not unheard of for an attorney to bill a client ten or twelve hours for that same three hours, arguing that that is his normal workday!

One firm that has taken travel billing to the level of an art is the Chicago firm of Sidley and Austin. In its 1987 defense of a lawsuit, Sidley billed the Bradley Trusts in Milwaukee $2.5 million, a chunk of which was for travel expenses. Even though Chicago is less than a two-hour drive from Milwaukee, Sidley attorneys preferred to fly, eventually billing Bradley $35,000 for airfare. Another entry on the Bradley bills was marked "Pfister Hotel 11/18-21 $9815.10." Four nights' lodging at $2453 a day? And that was just part of the hotel bill. The firm booked twelve hotel rooms for 112 nights, and one Sidley attorney billed Bradley for twenty-three meals, not in Milwaukee but in *Chicago*, ranging in price from $20 to $150.

Let's look at another technological marvel of the past forty years: the photocopy machine. Since its introduction to the business world, the photocopy machine has become a mistress for attorneys the world over—not a companion that is costly to keep, but one that turns a fat profit for its sponsor.

A standard photocopied page costs the owner of the machine between two and a half and three cents. Some attorneys and law firms absorb that cost, figuring it as part of their hourly fee, but frequently the cost is passed on to the client, with a slight adjustment for labor or machine maintenance. How slight? Anywhere from ten to fifty cents a page. With a profit margin of thirty-two cents a page, it does not take a rocket scientist to see the moneymaking possibilities. Suddenly, it becomes necessary to run off dozens of copies of an original document for circulation to consulting lawyers at the firm. Changes and revisions are made and dozens of copies are recirculated. After discussions with the client and the other side's attorneys, more revised copies are made and recirculated.

As an illustration of just what kind of moneymaking device a photocopying machine can be, a 1992 audit by Citicorp of its legal bills submitted by the New York law firm of Shearman and Sterling between 1989 and 1991 showed that the largest single item broken out on Shearman's bills was photocopying—a staggering $1.5 million, or 24 percent of all charges. And that was for only twelve legal matters Shearman had handled for Citicorp! Lawyers don't need a counterfeiting press to make money—they have photocopiers.

With the advent of the computer age, it became unnecessary for an attorney to waste precious hours drafting and dictating contracts and legal documents for a secretary or paralegal to type and retype. Now all one has to do is pull up the appropriate boilerplate forms, fill in the blanks, make minor modifications, and press the PRINT button. The client, of course, will be billed for every word in the contract, just as if they had all been written down with a quill pen. Billable hours in a computer chip.

Of course, even a word processor requires fingers to type a document onto a disk or to modify a document already stored. Up to ten years ago, in most cases those costs were included in an attorney's hourly rate. But during the 1980s, many firms saw a way to make extra money by breaking out these costs, and more and more clients began to find items for "secretarial overtime" and "night word processing" on their statements. The rationale used by the firms was that since they were providing their clients with an extra level of service, the client should pay for that service. If a secretary had to stay past five to type a document, why should the firm absorb the $50-an-hour, time-and-a-half cost?

Many big firms employ word processors who work through the night so that if a document is time-sensitive, the attorney can have it on his desk by morning. Only how many documents are so time-sensitive that they need to be produced overnight? And how is a client supposed to know if a secretary really stayed after five to do clerical work on his case?

In recent years, yet another miracle product was added to the lawyer's stock in trade to guarantee speed and efficiency: the fax machine. Again, some firms do not charge for telecopying documents, but most do, at a cost ranging from 50 cents to $3.50 a page, *plus* phone time. Not only do these firms charge for sending documents, they also charge for *receiving* them, sticking the client with a fee of two dollars or more a page for keeping their fax machine turned on.

Almost overnight, the postal service became a secondary means of document transmittal. Why send a document by mail when it can be faxed for three-fifty a page? Why indeed, in this miraculous age of communication? Legitimate? Yes. Ethical? That would depend on the circumstances. Again, aside from profit, how many valid reasons are there for instantaneous document transmittal?

Another technological innovation which has proven a gold mine for attorneys is the car phone. Now attorneys can rack up their billable hours on their way to and from the office, putting in calls to clients, secretaries, and other attorneys who may or may not yet be in their offices or are also in their cars, slogging through freeway traffic. Attorneys love to swap their car phone numbers. To most people, fighting freeway traffic on the way to work is a necessary drudgery. To an attorney, it's money-time. Permanent phone records are generated and the client *will* pay.

How much can all these incidentals add up to? Depending on the policies of the law firm, the sky can be the limit. The aforementioned 1992 Citicorp audit of Shearman and Sterling estimated that between 1989 and 1991 Citicorp had been overbilled *$57 million*. The largest single excessive charge the auditors found were items in which "professionals billed time for administrative-type activities." Among the charges that Shearman had broken out on its bills to Citicorp for twelve audited matters were:

| | |
|---|---|
| Word processing | $411,586 |
| Secretarial overtime | $212,720 |
| Facsimiles | $154,854 |
| Night services | $151,693 |
| Proofreading | $73,693 |

| | |
|---|---|
| Part-time help | $71,037 |
| Files retrieval | $1,113 |
| Conference rooms | $47,890 |
| Utilities | $29,500 |
| Leased Equipment | $24,914 |
| Velabinding | $9,642 |
| Stationery and supplies | $30,654 |
| In-house copies | $1,510,102 |
| Outside databases | $744,095 |
| In-house dining | $106,629 |
| Conference snacks | $4,063 |
| Outside client meals | $99,724 |
| Travel, air, hotel | $795,453 |
| Travel meals | $11,455 |

Despite the outrageous and astronomical charges listed in the audit, and despite Citicorp's complaints, Shearman & Sterling ended up refunding only $80,000 to the bank. It makes one wonder who else was billed for Shearman's utility bills, outside databases, in-house dining, conference rooms, and leased equipment—and *didn't* complain.

This "unbundling" of overhead charges has become alarmingly popular at many major law firms as partners and office managers have come to view every firm operation as an individual profit center. An example of how far this has gone took place in 1990 at a conference at the offices of New York's Skadden, Arps, Slate, Meagher and Flom. During a meeting with a client, the South Florida Water Management District, a Skadden senior associate thoughtfully ordered coffee, juice, and Danish for four from Skadden's in-house cafeteria. The Water Management District later received a bill for $33.60 for the food—$24 for the food itself with an additional 40 percent tacked on as a surcharge.

One wouldn't think that a firm like Skadden, which according to the "Am Law 100" survey charges between $135 to $415 an hour, plus premiums, and at which the average profits per partner in 1990 were $920,000, would be so greedy that it would need to gouge its clients through its food service, but overcharging for Danishes was just part of the picture. A Water Management District audit of the $6 million in bills submitted by Skadden uncovered charges for such expenses as 45 cents per minute for "print tending" (tending to documents as they run through printers), $45 an hour for "library staff," $32,523 to send late-working employees home by taxicab, and $42,386 for lawyers' meals. In the end, Skadden knocked $1.1 million off the Water District's bill, but insisted that its expenses were "generated in accordance with normal billing practices."

But the Golden Chutzpah Award for Expense Padding has to go to the attorneys for Los Angeles Police Department beating victim Rodney King. According to federal law, the loser of a civil rights suit has to reimburse the winner for fees and expenses. Among the $4.4 million in legal fees (King only received $3.8 million in damages) King's attorneys submitted to the City of Los Angeles were reading a newspaper article about the trial ($81.25), attending King's 1991 birthday party ($650), and accompanying King to see the film *Malcolm X* ($1,300). Popcorn in that theater was obviously expensive.

Now, you might say, "Why should I care how much insurance companies or banks or cities get overcharged on their legal bills? My insurance company screws me every month. They can afford it." Sure they can. Because they're passing their legal costs on to you. Everything you buy today—from a child's toy to a stepladder to an insurance policy—has built-in legal costs, which by 1994 had risen to 5 percent of the average corporate budget.

Furthermore, it isn't just giant corporations that get the legal shaft, although they might get it in bigger doses. *If a law firm bills a big company for photocopying, it is going to bill you for photocopying, too.* A 1991 cross-sectional survey of the

American Bar Association found that 38 percent of the 270 lawyers who responded admitted they "occasionally" billed clients for work not done, and 17 percent admitted they had charged more than one client for the same work. If close to half of the respondents were that unabashedly honest about their dishonesty, one might safely guess that at least some of the other 62 percent lied in their responses and that a significant percentage of those who didn't respond also occasionally—and perhaps frequently—overbilled clients.

The sad fact is that the billing abuses that have come to light as a result of client complaints are merely the tip of the dirty iceberg. Many more instances take place daily and are suffered silently, albeit perhaps grudgingly, by law firm clients. Part of the reason that companies and individual clients may not complain is that the bills they receive are often in the form of unintelligible, elaborately coded reams of computer printouts describing the daily charges of every lawyer working on the case. Often a businessperson does not have time to pore over the documents in detail, and when he does, he cannot make heads or tails of them.

Work descriptions are often pithy, brief, and vague. It is not uncommon to see a huge monetary amount attached to a label as uninformative and cryptic as "Trial prep," "Wrote memorandum," or "Professional services." How can a client complain about a charge when she can't tell what the charge is for?

Billing abuses became a hot topic in legal circles a few years ago, and much noise has been made about instituting alternative forms of billing. The most frequent argument for alternative billing is that hourly billing is a disincentive for efficiency, that it encourages delay and overcomplication, and that it puts all the risk on the client.

The new emphasis, proponents say, should be on results, not time. If a lawyer gets a quick, advantageous result for the client, he or she should be rewarded for it in the form of an extra payment. Likewise, if the attorney gets a bad and costly result, something should be knocked off the bill, the lawyer thus assuming some of the client's risk. This alternative form of billing has come to be euphemistically called "value billing," and since the late 1980s, it has been eagerly embraced by various members of the bar.

Attorneys, however, generally don't like risk, at least when it comes to getting paid, and attorneys who "value bill" usually do so in combination with an hourly rate, which serves as a solid floor on which the "value" stands. And it is not surprising that although a lawyer will frequently think he should be rewarded for his efforts, he will almost never think he should be docked. Value billing, then, becomes a license to steal.

The following is an example of value billing taken directly from one attorney's retainer agreement:

> Nothing in this agreement nor in any of our represen-
> tations to you, whether before or after your execution of
> this agreement, is to be construed by you as a promise
> or guarantee about the outcome or result of your
> matter. Our firm cannot and does not make any prom-
> ise or guarantee to you about the outcome or results of
> your matter, and any representations by us before or
> after your execution of this agreement are expressions
> of opinion only.
>
> Moreover, you understand that our firm's billing
> system is based upon value, and not upon the number
> of hours expended. Hours simply are a convenient
> beginning point from which our firm calculates the
> final charges to a client. Therefore, the firm's charges
> for legal services are based upon more than our normal
> hourly rates. The final charge for our professional legal
> services may vary from our normal hourly rates be-
> cause of the existence of the following factors:
>
> 1. the complexity of the matter;
> 2. the time pressure under which the professional
> legal services were performed;

3. the amount of responsibility assumed by the firm;

4. the extent to which the professional legal services precluded other employment;

5. the amount involved in the matter;

6. the nature and length of the firm's relationship with the client;

7. the efficiency with which the professional legal services were performed;

8. the nature of the professional legal services provided;

9. the results we achieved.

Hence, depending upon the presence of some or all of these factors, our normal hourly charges may be reduced or increased by as much as fifteen percent (15%).

Now let's try to analogize this to the normal business world. You check into a hotel and are told by the desk clerk that a double room will be $50. You agree to the rate and secure the room with your credit card (your retainer). After you have paid and gotten a receipt, you are given your room key, along with a sheet of paper that explains that for $50, the hotel is not guaranteeing that your room will be reasonably clean, that the TV or toilets will work, or that you will be happy with the room you get. You are also told that $50 may or may not even *be* the rate of your room, that the final determination of what you will eventually pay will depend on:

1. how complicated it was to find you a room;

2. how quickly the hotel had to locate a room;

3. the amount of responsibility the hotel is willing to assume;

4. the extent to which providing you a room kept the hotel from renting a room to someone else;

5. how much you are willing to pay for the room;

6. how frequently you stay at the hotel and how often;

7. how efficient the hotel's desk clerks and maids are;

8. what kind of services the hotel provides; and

9. your degree of happiness with the room and service.

You are furthermore told that after all those variables are considered, you will be notified of what the real room charge will be—at the time you check out!

Needless to say, a person would have to be an idiot to stay at such a hotel, and any hotel that tried to conduct business in such a way would be closed in a month. It is perhaps the ultimate irony that an attorney would urge a client to sign what no half-smart attorney would ever advise a client to sign under any circumstances—and to sign what in the business world would possibly subject him to a malpractice suit. The only assumption can be that value-billing attorneys aren't half-smart, but assume their clients *are*.

The American Bar Association, always concerned about the complaints of clients about being overbilled by attorneys, is vigilant in its search for creative alternatives to hourly billing. In its continuing education programs, the ABA offers seminars, tapes, and literature that help its members keep up with the newest trends in alternative billing.

One such book, offered through the catalog of the Law Practice Management Section of the Bar, is called *Beyond the Billable Hour: An Anthology of Alternative Billing Methods* and is available to members at a mere $65. Advertised as "the landmark book that set the stage for the whole discussion on value billing," the book discusses some of the newer billing methods, such as "cost-plus" (plus whatever the lawyer wants to add onto the bill), "punitive billing" (as if lawyers' bills weren't punitive enough), and "de Sade billing" (supposedly where the lawyer tortures the client into paying).

With the ABA not merely sanctioning "creative billing," but offering its members *instruction* on its methods, it's no wonder that lawyers take liberties with their bills.

"It's not that these lawyers are crooks," say legal billing critics Susan Beck and Michael Orey. "The trouble is more deep-seated than that. These firms actually think these charges are fair and represent good management, and they pass them on with a sense of entitlement, not apology.

"The cost to the client is more than just dollars. The need to be vigilant in guarding against such charges undermines the trust that should be at the core of a lawyer-client relationship."

# 4

# The Big Stall: A Modern Fairy Tale About Lawyers and the American Dream

Once upon a time there was a man named Fred Griffith.*
Fred had always had a passion for cars, and after graduating
from high school, he got a job in the parts department of a
large southern California Chevy dealership. A very bright and
capable young man, Fred soon worked his way up to manager
of that department, went to General Motors school where he
learned to be a master mechanic, and eventually ended up as
the dealer's sales manager. His dream, however, was to get a
"point," a dealership of his own.

At the annual GM convention, he discussed his dream
with the GM district manager, who was impressed with Fred's
eagerness and advised him to start out with a used car lot. If
he operated that successfully for a couple of years, the district

---

*Asterisks denote pseudonyms.

manager promised he would get him his dealership.

Fred refinanced his home for $75,000, then went to an independent banker he knew and established a line of credit. He bought used cars from the wholesale auction and used the cars' titles to collateralize the loans.

Everything went along nicely for a year. The operation was profitable, Fred was paying his bills, and he was convinced his "point" was just around the corner. Then he made the biggest mistake of his life—he sold Philip Wernicke* a 1989 Buick.

Wernicke, an argumentative individual who, unbeknownst to Fred, had a penchant for suing people, was back the next day with the complaint that the Buick's tires shimmied at 50 mph. Fred had the tires balanced at no charge. The next day, Wernicke was in Fred's office saying the problem was worse than ever. Fred put a new set of tires on the car.

During the following weeks, Wernicke returned the car for repairs on its electric windows, its electric seat control, and its "rough-running engine," all of which Fred fixed apologetically.

For a while, all was quiet and Fred thought he had solved his customer's problems. That fantasy was dispelled when Wernicke called and accused Fred of fraud and misrepresentation. It seemed that records showed that the '89 Buick was originally sold in 1988. Fred offered Wernicke his money back, but Wernicke refused, demanding $5,000 *and* the car. Fred refused and the next day was served with a complaint asking for $1,000,000 for fraud, misrepresentation, intentional infliction of emotional distress, and punitive damages.

Upset, Fred took the complaint to his lawyer, who dismissed the seriousness of the charges and told him not to worry—he would call Wernicke's attorney and find out what Wernicke really wanted to settle the matter.

The following day, Fred's attorney informed him that Wernicke now wanted $25,000 to go away, and suggested they file an answer to the complaint. He predicted that the cost of the case would be minimal and that their chances of winning were favorable. At the same time, he informed Fred that a state statute did contain a provision that a car dealer had to pay his customer's attorney's fees if the customer was awarded so much as $1 in damages. But the case was simple, so what could that amount to?

Fred's attorney filed a three-page answer denying the accusation and laying out Fred's version of the events. Wernicke's attorney fired back a motion to strike the affirmative defense, which the judge granted. Nine months later, after all efforts to settle the case were rejected by the plaintiff, a three-day trial ensued resulting in a $1,000 award to Wernicke on the basis that the Buick had indeed first been sold in 1988. Fred was also instructed to pay Wernicke's legal fees, which amounted to $89,300. Fred's own attorney, in a magnanimous gesture, reduced his own legal fees by one-third, charging Fred only $27,000. Since Fred's insurance didn't cover "fraud," Fred had to pay the entire amount himself.

Two weeks later, Fred handed the keys to his business to another used car dealer and received a check for $80,000. His hope of getting his dealership dead, he ended up working in sales at his old employer, the Chevy dealership.

Fred Griffith's case is a perfect illustration of how attorneys employ dilatory and obstructionist tactics to run up their bills. Lawyers are like Paris taxi drivers—once they've got you in the cab and the meter is running, they'll always take the longest way to get you where you're going. And the circuitous routes they use are innumerable. Let's take a look at just a few.

### Writs and Motions

The due process clause of the U.S. Constitution has been interpreted to mean that no legal proceeding can take place without one side of a lawsuit giving the other "proper and timely" notice. This process begins when a plaintiff institutes a lawsuit by filing a complaint in the clerk's office and serving a summons on the defendant.

As the case winds its way tortuously through the court system, each attorney is required to give opposing counsel notice of every court maneuver he intends to take which might adversely affect the other side of the controversy. Notice must be given of all motions which are made, such as demurrers, motions for summary judgment, motions to compel answers, motions to strike, and dozens of other tactics only lawyers can contrive.

For the purpose of ruling on writs and motions, the judiciary has created departments known as "law and motion." In a busy law and motion department, it is not unusual to have twenty-five to thirty cases set for a three-hour morning calendar. One judge can easily handle that caseload because he and his staff spend several hours reviewing the moving and opposing papers and arriving at a tentative ruling. Armed with the research, the judge spends only an average of five minutes listening to the lawyers argue their points of law. It is rare that tentative rulings are changed and, as a practical matter, the attorneys could call the clerk the day before the scheduled hearing, get a tentative ruling, and submit the case without even appearing in court. Few do, however. Why? Because that way, they wouldn't be able to rack up those billable hours.

On law and motion day, lawyers who are engaged in trial at the time or are required to make an appearance in another courtroom get priority to go to the head of the line. Once the priority cases are ruled upon, those with the shortest time estimates are next taken up; the longer the argument, the later the case is heard. The idea behind this procedure is to enable busy lawyers to get back to their offices. Only most of the time, they don't. Briefcases in hand, the friendly enemies will exit the courtroom together and adjourn to the cafeteria, where discussion of the case is sandwiched between more important subject matter: the Super Bowl, the World Series, the Masters' Tournament, or whatever sporting event is timely. And all the while, the meter continues to run and the billable hours mount—three hours of court time, an hour driving to court and an hour driving back to the office. If the lawyer has been successful in scheduling three cases on the same day, regardless of the outcomes of the motions, he will leave the courthouse with a particular sense of accomplishment in that he can bill all three clients five hours each. If he takes along an associate he doesn't really need, he can bill for that lawyer's time, too.

There are lawyers—and not just a few of them—who do nothing but file frivolous motions so they can bill for the court time. It matters little that their motions will almost assuredly be denied and that the client's case has not been helped. It's another way to get into the client's pocketbook.

An attorney doesn't even have to file purposeless motions with the court to make money. All he has to do is prepare them. The Los Angeles law firm of Gibson, Dunn and Crutcher was recently rebuked by an Oakland judge for overcharging $600,000 in the handling of a corporate bankruptcy reorganization. Part of the fees the firm requested, but which were disallowed by the judge, were for motions and suits that were *prepared but not filed*. Even *after* the major parties had agreed to a reorganization plan, the Gibson lawyers kept the meter running by working on an objection to confirmation of the plan!

In addition to the more technical legal motions, lawyers frequently make motions for continuances, that is, to put off the case in court to a later date. Such motions are usually made because of "scheduling conflicts"—for instance, if one attorney or the other is trying a case in another court at the same time as the case at hand. Most attorneys don't object to granting the opposition's motions for continuance, due to the fact that they regularly have scheduling conflicts also. It is referred to in the trade as "professional courtesy." In reality, scheduling conflicts can be for reasons other than trial dates—namely, weddings, bar mitzvahs, vacations, and golf games. Having husbands or wives, children and golf buddies, too, judges are usually very understanding about such conflicts and rarely deny such motions. They will generally schedule hearings at a "mutually convenient time" for attorneys.

In Fred's case, Wernicke's attorney's charges for preparation of pleadings and motions—motions to strike, motions to depose, motions for continuances, motions to compel answers, review and preparation of responses to motions—totaled $7,950. Fred's attorney only charged $3,200.

### Discovery

"Discovery" literally means "the disclosure of that which was previously hidden." The rule of discovery in American law refers to the disclosure by the defendant of facts, deeds, or documents that are in someone's exclusive possession and that are necessary to the suing party in order to get at the truth. Aside from helping the court uncover the truth behind a lawsuit, a side effect of discovery is supposed to be to facilitate dispute settlement.

The reasoning here is that if one side to a lawsuit learns everything about his or her opponent's case, reasonably prudent people will have an incentive to settle their differences without taking the matter to trial. A nice theory. In practice, however, the rule has been subverted by lawyers and turned into a veritable cash cow, to the point where American companies spend up to *80 percent of their legal bills on discovery*.

The discovery rule was intended to enable one side of a dispute to gain access to information pertinent to the case at hand. Lawyers, however, always looking for inventive ways to make a buck, frequently use discovery indiscriminately by gathering up unneeded volumes of information to enable them to sift laboriously through unrelated documents at $300 an hour. At least clients are billed as if they had sifted through them.

In many of these cases, particularly involving large corporations, the documents collected are never read by the discovering attorneys. Estimates of how long it would take to go through the material are made and charged to clients as "research." The documents are stored, however, just in case the client wants some corroboration for all this "research." It's not the lawyer's fault that nothing was found in the documents that could be used to advance the client's case.

Too often today, lawyers are using discovery rules not to find the facts, but to force a financially weaker opponent to surrender by making costly demands for documents and voluminous and often unnecessary interviews of possible witnesses.

As Harvard Law Professor Arthur Miller puts it, the discovery system is out of control, permitting "artful attorneys to hide the ball and keep alive hopeless claims as well as defenses...In many ways, [it] is analogous to the dance marathon contests of yesteryear. The object of the exercise is to...hang on to one's client, and then drift aimlessly and endlessly to the litigation music for as long as possible, hoping that everyone else will collapse from exhaustion."

How accepted these practices have become was illustrated at Stanford University when one of the partners at Cravath, Swaine, and Moore bragged to an audience of law students that he could take the "simplest antitrust case and protract for the defense almost to infinity. [One case] lasted fourteen years...Despite 50,000 pages of testimony, there really wasn't any dispute about the facts...We won that case, and as you know, my firm's meter was running all the time—every month for fourteen years." In a more recent case, IBM was ordered by the court to produce documents for examination by the plaintiff that totaled 64,000,000 pages!

Fred, by comparison, got off easy. His bill for discovery, including "review and research of documents," only came to $5,700.

### Interrogatories

This is a fancy legal term for "written questions." After an answer to a complaint has been filed, the first set of "interogs," as they are commonly called, is served on opposing counsel by mail, along with instructions on how to provide the answers. Answers to these questions are required generally twenty to thirty days after mailing.

Interogs can be very complex, containing not only questions, but sub-questions and sub-questions to the sub-questions, *ad nauseam*. But what is nauseating to you is not necessarily nauseating to an attorney. On the contrary. Attorneys *love* interrogatories, because once the plaintiff's questions are received, defense counsel can fire off his own interogs, often identical to the plaintiff's. This inevitably leads to second, third, and fourth sets of interogs being mailed back and forth, and the cash continues to flow.

Law book publishers, in their never-tiring quest to feed lawyers' need for billable hours, have produced volumes of books containing sample interrogatories in every field. Many are now available on computer disk, so all the lawyer has to do is punch a few buttons and presto, hundreds of questions with numerous sub-parts magically appear. While the production may take minutes, the client is billed for hours of review and preparation.

Even if the attorney spends five hours making up his own set of interrogatories, what he will then typically do is send out that same set to all the parties involved and charge the client for *each set sent out*, thus turning a five-hour job into a fifty-hour billing bonanza.

The right to send interrogatories is not absolute or endless. The respondent has the right to object to the questions put to him or her for any number of reasons. Objections, of course, are appreciated because the lawyer sending the interogs can then file a motion to compel the other side to answer. These motions are supported by affidavits and declarations and a legal brief entitled "Points and Authorities." Lots of hours can be billed for this exercise. In fact, a typical tactic by attorneys employed by the defense is to interpose objections to every point made by the plaintiff's side in order to slow things down and squeeze every possible billable hour from the courtroom proceeding.

In Fred's case, he was forced to answer interrogatories about the details of the transaction; the Buick's history (of which Fred had no knowledge, including its previous owners, and how much was paid for the car every time it changed hands); the names, addresses, and telephone numbers of every person who had purchased a car from Fred together with the make, model, and serial number of each vehicle and the amount paid for it; a list of all banks and finance companies with which he had ever done business; and a customer list for the last two years. He was also required to supply his financial statements. (Although Fred's attorney argued that supplying financial information as requested was an invasion of privacy, the judge ruled that since punitive damages were being asked for, it was necessary to determine Fred's net worth in order to judge the amount that would be awarded, if any.) Plaintiff's attorney's fees for preparation and review of interrogatories: $7,900. Fred's attorney: $2,250.

## Depositions

A deposition is the examination of a witness under oath and in the presence of a court reporter, who takes down the questions and answers and types them into a document called a transcript.

There are several ways that an attorney can abuse the deposition process. One is to depose everybody in sight, whether or not he is likely to have seen or heard anything pertinent to the case. In medical malpractice cases, for example, depositions will typically be taken of every doctor, nurse, orderly, technician, clerk, or janitor whose name appears in the medical records or who was on duty on the day of the incident in question. It doesn't matter that the person deposed worked in a different ward or a different floor, or had no contact with the patient filing the malpractice case or the doctor being sued. The rationale is that there's a *chance* somebody saw something.

The second typical way an attorney can run up the tab for depositions is by asking pages of questions only marginally related to the issue at hand instead of focusing on the two or three questions pertinent to the client's case. Thus he turns what should have been a half-hour deposition into two or three hours.

Mr. Wernicke's attorney, in an attempt to get at the "truth" of his client's case, deposed Fred's bookkeeper, mechanics, secretary, receptionist, bankers, and sixteen of his customers, all of whom expressed satisfaction in their dealings with Fred. He also employed and deposed a forensic accountant, who combed through Fred's financial records, searching for inconsistencies and, more important, assets on which to base his punitive claims. Cost: $15,400.

Not all inflated deposition costs are incurred by the attorney; some are due to the practices of deposition services hired by attorneys to transcribe witness testimony. In nearly all states deposition reporters get paid by the page and they have a number of tricks to drive up the cost of depositions, including using larger type, wide margins, and larger spaces between lines and paragraphs.

By these methods, a service can easily add ten extra pages to a 200-page deposition, as well as use those pages as justification for charging an extra hour or two at its billable rate. It means nothing to the attorney, of course. These extra charges are just passed on to the client.

Your lawyer might tell you that he's not making a dime off you for these depositions, that you are merely repaying him for money he has already laid out to the service. That may or may not be true. Deposition services often offer attorneys 10 percent discounts if their bill is paid within ten days. That discount is a bookkeeping entry between the lawyer and the service and often does not find its way onto a client's bill. Thus, the service may charge a lawyer $400 for a job and receive $360 from the lawyer as a reward for prompt payment, while the lawyer pockets $40 of the client's money. Such practices give an incentive to the greedy lawyer to use regularly a service that not only gives such discounts but is also the most expensive.

### Mandatory Settlement Conferences

Most courts in America have established a mandatory settlement conference (MSC) during which both sides and their attorneys are required to appear before a judge to discuss the ramifications of the case. The judge will then attempt to coerce a disposition. Unfortunately, these MSCs are ordinarily held *after* discovery has been completed and huge attorney's fees have piled up.

Similarly, courts of appeal establish settlement conferences, but only after briefs have been filed and extensive legal fees have been charged. If judges would schedule MSCs *before* discovery and *before* appellate briefing, clients would save considerable expense, but lawyers would be very unhappy. Fred's case illustrates why.

After a three-hour settlement conference involving Wernicke's attorney, his assistant attorney, and Fred's attorney, the plaintiff refused to settle and the case proceeded to trial. The combined attorneys' fees for "review notice of MSC," "preparation for MSC," "conference with client about MSC," "telephone call with client about MSC," "consultation with assistant counsel about MSC," "office conferences with client regarding settlement of MSC," "appearance at MSC," and "post MSC consultation with client": $5,300.

Add to all that the cost for telephone calls between the opposing attorneys, other consultations with the client's preparation for trial, and the trial itself, and Freddy's nightmare moved from Elm Street into his home.

The moral of the fairy tale: The American Dream is still alive and well for lawyers, but, once they start their clocks, dicey for the rest of us.

# PART II

## HOW TO MINIMIZE THE HURT

# 5

## Picking the Right Attorney

The biggest mistake most people make in dealing with attorneys is picking the wrong one. And picking the wrong attorney is a lot easier than picking the right one. Probably eighty percent of all attorneys practicing law shouldn't be, so you're starting out with an eight-out-of-ten chance your choice will be incompetent. Of the other twenty percent, some are good for particular jobs, but not for others. A Harvard-educated business attorney might be just what you need to structure a corporate merger, but in a criminal courtroom he or she would probably get carved up like a Christmas turkey.

But before you go out and hire an attorney to represent you, you must first answer a more fundamental question: Do you need an attorney at all? If the answer is "I'm not sure," you could be getting ready to flush a pile of money down the toilet for nothing. If you don't absolutely *need* to hire an attorney, our advice is *don't*. Pause, relax, take a deep breath, and consider your alternatives.

## 1. Define the Nature of Your Problem

Is it a personal problem, a business problem, or a legal problem? Or is it a business or personal problem that could turn into a legal problem, such as a divorce?

A lawyer should never be allowed to make a personal or business decision for you. Remember, once an attorney is in the game, it's in his interest to turn your personal problem into a legal one.

## 2. Try Talking to the Other Side

Once involved, attorneys will always try to keep you from talking to the other participant in your situation, whether it be a divorce, business dispute, contract negotiation, or criminal matter. In the last instance, the advice is totally sound. In the others, it may or may not be.

Attorneys try to choke off communication between clients by rationalizing that it is their professional duty to shelter you from grief and annoyances generated by the other side. In reality, it's just a control game. As long as an attorney can choke off dialogue and know more about the situation than you do, he is in control.

It has often been observed that the only participants who win in litigation are the attorneys. So before you get one, try talking to the other side to see if you can work things out. Determine what you will accept in the way of a settlement. Do this by putting down on a piece of paper what you want, then subtracting what you estimate your legal fees will be if you have to go to litigation. If the other side is willing to give you a solution in between those two figures, take it and run like hell.

## 3. Go to Arbitration

If the other side is amenable, the cost of arbitrating or mediating a dispute can be minimal when compared to getting a case before a judge. In mediation, the parties in dispute are called together by a neutral third party, such as a judge, who takes input from both sides and makes recommendations for working out a settlement. In arbitration, the neutral third party does not have discussions with either side, but considers the evidence submitted to him or her from both sides and renders a judgment, either binding or nonbinding, to dispose of the case. Arbitration is often included as a first step in many business contracts, and is widely used in construction disputes, litigation, and property settlements, such as in a divorce proceeding.

Although there are professional arbitrators who list their services in the yellow pages, the best and least expensive service is the American Arbitration Association (AAA), which has been in existence for over fifty years. Most of the arbitrators who work through the AAA are unpaid professionals who are experts in their particular field. In a construction dispute, for instance, the arbitration panel might consist of a general contractor, an architect, and a structural engineer. A computer software rights dispute might draw a computer programmer and a patent attorney.

Another competent firm, based in Orange County, California, is Judicial Arbitration and Mediation Services, Inc. (JAMS). JAMS has eighteen offices in four states staffed by 175 former judges who handle 14,000 cases a year. The cost is between $300 and $350 an hour, but the average case is resolved in days or, sometimes, hours. Aside from the fact that it is more expensive than the AAA, another significant disadvantage to JAMS in our opinion is that some of the judges who are supplementing their pensions by doing JAMS work are elderly—some extremely so—and not at their former mental or professional peak.

### 4. Use Paralegals

If your legal matter is uncomplicated, and nonadversarial, and primarily involves filling out and filing legal forms and answering "Yes" and "No" in front of a judge, you might consider having a paralegal do the job.

Paralegals are professional legal assistants who usually got their training in law offices as legal secretaries or researchers. Many graduated from law school but failed to pass the state bar exam. Some states, like Texas, have created legal assistants' divisions, which require the paralegal to pass an examination plus have at least one year's experience as a legal assistant under an attorney's supervision. Other states have no such stringent requirements, and states in which the bar has a stranglehold over the legal process outlaw the profession of paralegals working independently of an attorney's office as the "unauthorized practice of law." In Illinois, for example, both sides involved in a real estate transaction *must* be represented by an attorney, while in California and a growing number of states, title companies and escrow agents who may or may not be paralegals specializing in real property transactions are recognized as competent to draft and execute such documents.

Where they are allowed to practice, paralegals commonly handle such matters as uncontested divorce, bankruptcy, evictions and landlord services, guardianships, probate, simple wills, debt counseling, incorporation, adoptions, real estate transfers, living trusts, and small claims procedures.

Paralegals cannot offer legal advice, however. You must tell them what you want done and they will follow the proper procedures, fill out the correct legal documents, and instruct you how and when to file the paperwork. So you have to know going in exactly what you need to accomplish.

We know many paralegals who are experienced, thorough, and capable. Furthermore, since paralegals are constantly under fire from bar associations which are trying to stifle the competition, if they err, it will frequently be on the side of caution.

If you are considering hiring a paralegal, first check out

what professional requirements exist in your state. You can find this out by calling your local bar association. If there are none, be careful. Because it is a lucrative and fast-growing industry, many people billing themselves as "legal assistants" are nothing more than secretary-typists with little or no legal training.

If you have an attorney friend you trust, ask for a recommendation. He or she will more than likely know which paralegals in town do good work. A court reporter or private investigator might also be able to steer you in the right direction.

If you're hiring blind, look in the yellow pages under "Paralegals" or "Legal Clinics," and start phoning. Ask the paralegal what experience he has had, the names of any attorneys he worked for and for how long, and how long he has been on his own. Also ask if he can give you the names of attorneys who would be willing to give a reference.

And remember: If your legal matter is complex or adversarial, involves a lot of money, or poses serious ramifications for you, think twice about saving the money and get an attorney.

## Now You Need a Lawyer

So all of your other options are exhausted, and you have determined you need an attorney. How do you find one who is going to get the job done for you?

Here are some reasons *not* to hire a particular attorney:

- Because he's your cousin Vinny.
- Because he/she's on the treadmill next to yours at the gym every morning.
- Because he/she handled an entirely different kind of case for someone you know.
- Because he/she belongs to your Rotary Club and is personable.

- Because he/she was on TV last night at three in the morning, between the 900 hotlines, telling you what a wonderful job he/she will do for you.
- Because his/her office is down the hall from yours.

The law is becoming more and more specialized every day, so it is *imperative that you find someone competent and experienced who suits your needs.* Some areas of law are highly specialized, however, and some are not. Many more attorneys are capable of competently handling a personal injury, family law, or residential real estate case, for example, than are capable of dealing with the complexities of corporate, copyright, or environmental law. The key in any legal matter in which you may find yourself embroiled is to *find a lawyer who handles your kind of case on a regular basis.*

### Personal Referrals

The best place to start is getting a recommendation from someone you know with good judgment. Attorneys know the competition. If you know one, or several, call them up and ask whom they would hire if they had a problem like yours. Try calling those attorneys who specialize in fields different from your case. That way you have a tactful way out if the attorney tries to tout himself for the job.

You might also try surveying judges, court reporters, and other people who have been around the courts and seen various attorneys work. Make a broad inquiry of friends and business associates to find out if any of them have had a similar problem and got satisfactory results from their attorney. If they lost their cases, get the names of the other sides' attorneys.

In the course of your inquiries, you will probably find people advising you to stay away from lawyers A, B, and C. When you get a negative or positive response, ask the reasons for it, then independently make your own evaluation. Lawyer

A might have a terrible bedside manner and may not be a very likable guy, but you aren't looking for a soul mate, only someone who can get you what you want.

## Bar Association Referral Services

Many bar associations across the country have created lawyers' referral services, which are committees of volunteer attorneys who offer initial client interviews for a nominal fee (around $50). If you have a legal question you want answered about a point of law or a legal decision (Do I need an attorney to handle this matter? Do I have a case? Do I need a specialist?), this might be a good, cheap place to call. The lawyer should also have a list of qualified attorneys who are certified specialists in a particular area of law. If the attorney tries to tout himself for your job, tell him you'll think about it (don't) and get some other names.

These referral services can usually be found in the yellow pages under Attorneys' Referral Services. If you can't find a listing there, look in the white pages under the name of your local bar association. If there isn't a separate listing for the referral service, call the bar association's main number for information.

*When you call, make sure you are talking to a bar-sponsored referral service.* Just as there are dental referral services subsidized by dentists, there are private legal referral services that get paid by lawyers for a listing. They aren't about to tell you that a lawyer who's paying their phone bill is a moron, as he well might be.

## Martindale-Hubbell

Published since 1868, this reference guide is a listing of lawyers by geographical area, giving their specialization, sometimes a brief biography, including where they attended law school, and, often, a rating. The data, including the ratings, are compiled through polls of attorneys in the com-

munity and rate how an attorney's peers judge his or her
ability, experience, and honesty. The directory is updated
annually and is available at most public libraries or at law
libraries.

The ratings are "A" (very high), "B" (high), and "C" (fair).
There may be no rating, which may not mean anything, as we
will explain. The attorney's standard of ethics is also rated, by
a "V" next to his or her name. Thus, an "AV" rating is the top
rating an attorney can get. The absence of a "V" again does not
necessarily mean the lawyer is a crook or of questionable
character.

Why we say that absence of a rating might not mean
anything is that because the ratings are given by a lawyer's
peers, friendships and political allegiances can play a major
part in whether an attorney gets an "A" or a "C." Most large
firms *always* get "AV" ratings because of their size. In
addition, some very competent lawyers don't want to be rated,
so they aren't. It is, however, a good reference to check out,
and we know a lot of very qualified attorneys who flatly state
they themselves would not hire an attorney who had less than
a "BV" rating.

### Pre-Paid Legal Plans

These plans, analogous to health maintenance organizations (HMOs) in the medical field, have historically been
available through credit or trade unions, but more recently
through credit card companies like American Express. They
are paid for through nominal monthly payroll deductions or
subscriber fees. Their advantage is that they are inexpensive.
Their disadvantage is that you get what you pay for. The
monthly fees usually cover only limited telephone conversations and perhaps a few other services, such as letter-
writing. Still, such a service might be of value if you have a
simple question you want answered or if you want advice on
how to *prevent* a legal situation from occurring.

Two sources of information on such plans are:

National Resource Center for Consumers of Legal Services
Tabb House
Main Street
P.O. Box 340
Gloucester, VA 23061

American Pre-Paid Legal Services Institute
541 N. Fairbanks Court
Chicago, IL 60611

## The Yellow Pages

Your telephone directory will undoubtedly have an abundance of attorney listings and advertisements. After the alphabetized listings, it might also break down the lawyers under legal specialties. *Be careful here.* Just because a lawyer pays for a listing under a particular specialty doesn't mean he is a specialist in that field.

In some states, like California, lawyers who wish to be recognized as specialists by the bar have to qualify for certification by accumulating a minimum amount of experience in a particular field. Very few of the ads you will see in the yellow pages will say "Certified Specialist" under the lawyer's name. Even if a lawyer is certified, it doesn't mean he's any good. We've known certified specialists who have lost every case they've tried. But at least you know the specialist has some court time under his belt, which is more than can be said for most practicing attorneys.

One type of attorney to avoid at all costs is the one who proclaims himself to be competent in all areas of law. An attorney who claims to be a jack of all trades is usually the master of none. Go through the listings. If you find the same lawyer advertising under the divorce, personal injury, bankruptcy, immigration, business, and criminal headings, cross him off your list of possibilities. He's just a B.S. artist who's trying to reel in the maximum number of clients.

## Lawyer Pools

Some lawyers, particularly in the personal injury field, have set up referral hotlines which are advertised on TV, often with a celebrity endorsing the product. One such hotline, "Lawyers Direct," has ex-football star and actor Alex Karras warning viewers, "When you get into an accident, you can't afford to lose," and telling them to call an 800 number for help.

These advertisements are paid for by lawyers who have pooled their money and take cases on a rotational basis. *They are not independent referral services*, any more than the dental or doctor referral services you see on TV are. They are a grab-bag, and as the man says, "You pays your money and you takes your chances." Needless to say, choosing an attorney by drawing lots is tremendously risky, analogous to blindfolding yourself and playing pin the tail on the attorney. Contrary to what Mr. Karras says, if you can't afford to lose, be wary of 800 numbers.

## Narrowing Your Possibilities

Say you now have a list of possibilities. To narrow the field further, telephone the state bar and ask if any of the people on your list have ever been disciplined for ethical or legal misconduct. If the clerk on the other end of the line refuses to give you the information, remind him or her about the Freedom of Information Act. Disciplinary actions by the bar are public information and you are entitled to it.

Go down to the local county courthouse and go through the civil case index to see if the attorney has ever been involved in a lawsuit as a plaintiff or, more important, as a defendant. Find out if he's ever been sued by a client for malpractice or overcharging or if he was dilatory in his actions, resulting in a default judgment against any of his clients. If he has been and lost, you might want to save yourself possible grief and make another choice. Even if he hasn't lost, but has been sued more than once, it's a good indication the lawyer might be dishonest or incompetent. Speaking of dishonesty, while you're at the courthouse, you might also comb the criminal court index to see if the attorney has ever been charged with a crime. If so, scratch his or her name off your list.

In making your final selection, take into account your opposition. Is the other side (whether it be a businessperson, ex-spouse, employee, etc.) susceptible to a certain kind of approach? Is he sensitive, irascible, contentious? Does she hate to be hassled, bullied, threatened? How does he react when threatened? Does he cave? Maybe you want a nasty trench-fighter attorney. Is she susceptible to the rational approach? Try an attorney with a more businesslike manner. Does he hate to spend money? Find a procrastinator, who will cost your opponent a fortune in time and money by delay, depositions, and discovery.

One primary factor should go into your choice of lawyer, and that is the size of the firm the lawyer works for. Never hire a major firm unless you like wasting money on the firm's overhead and the huge salaries of its senior partners. If you do hire a big firm, chances are you'll have to hire a second lawyer to keep the big firm from doing so many unnecessary tasks to rack up billable hours. If your matter does end up in court, it will be handled by the large firm's litigation department. Often, litigators who work for large firms have tried no more than ten cases in a twenty-year career. Many senior partners have not seen the inside of a courtroom in that same twenty years.

Our recommendation is to go with either a small firm (two or more partners, plus a couple of associates) or a single practitioner. Much of the time, small firm partners started out working for larger firms, got disgruntled and frustrated seeing all the money being raked off by less talented senior partners, and broke away on their own. A small firm has an advantage over a single practitioner in that partners usually have different talents, e.g., researcher versus litigator. They can also discuss the case with each other and share ideas.

Single practitioners have the advantage of familiarity. For some people, that's very important; for others, it's not. In certain matters like bankruptcy, probate, criminal, or divorce, a single practitioner, *if he or she's good*, can usually work out fine. If your legal problem is of a complex, big business nature, however, a lone wolf attorney may not be the way you want to go. He may lack the expertise or the resources to call upon in a pinch.

Stay local. Not only will you be saving yourself several hundred dollars an hour in attorneys' traveling time, you are paying for a firm that has a degree of accountability to the community. Many attorneys are active in service clubs and social and political affairs. They also know the judges.

Two types of lawyers are generally looked upon with disdain by local judges—advertising lawyers and out-of-town representatives of big-gun, high-rent firms who appear in local courts with an attitude of superiority. The old sports cliché, "It was a hometown decision," can also apply in a court of law. A good local attorney who has appeared before a judge many times before knows what that judge wants to hear, how he wants motions made, and how he operates his courtroom.

So now you've made your selection—a small, local firm with a good reputation. It's time to find out if it's the right one.

### The First Interview

When you show up at the attorney's office, scope out the digs. What is the office overhead like? Is the office unpretentious, businesslike? Or is it a plush seventeenth-floor suite in an expensive high-rise building? Don't harbor any illusions: You're going to be paying for the office furniture.

When you are ushered into the inner sanctum and meet the man or woman you are there to see, lay out your problem as candidly and succinctly as possible. (You might want to put it in writing for yourself before you go there to make sure you aren't leaving out any salient points.) Don't try to slant your arguments in your favor or leave out any of the bad points of your case. Just give the lawyer as many of the facts as you can as objectively as you can. *This is not the time to hold anything back.*

This is also not the time for holding back questions, as shy as you may be. That joker sitting across the desk is shortly going to do some serious dipping into your bank account, and before you give him the go-ahead, you deserve to know who he is, what he expects to be able to do for you, and how serious the dipping is going to be.

Some absolutely vital questions to ask:

1. *How experienced is the lawyer in handling matters like yours?* How many has she handled in the past? How successful were the outcomes? If it is going to involve a trial, how many court trials has the lawyer handled in the past two years? (Less than 10 percent of licensed lawyers try more than half a dozen cases in their entire careers.) What were the outcomes of the trials?

2. *Do you have a case?* Is it worth pursuing? What are the chances of victory? (A lot of lawyers will balk at estimating chances, but if yours knows his law and the way similar court decisions have been going, he might give you a ballpark guess, like 75–25 or 60–40.) If you score a victory, will it be a Pyrrhic one? What is the downside? Are you likely to wind up spending more in legal fees than you can get in a settlement?

3. *Who will be handling your case?* Will the lawyer of your choice handle it personally, or will he turn it over to an

associate or one of his paralegals? This is *very important*. If the attorney tries to give you the brush at this point by turning you over to one of his office flunkies, get up and walk out. Your case is important to you; if it isn't to him, he isn't the lawyer you want.

4. *How does he charge?* By the hour, flat fee, or contingency? If he charges by the hour, what is his hourly rate and that of his paralegals or secretaries? (Take heed: Just because the lawyer charges a fortune doesn't mean you will end up spending more. An unscrupulous or incompetent lawyer who charges $150 an hour and takes three months to settle your case will end up costing more than a $400-an-hour guy who gets the job done in one.)

If he is charging a flat fee and the first interview is free (you can determine this by a pre-meeting phone call), you may want to make similar appointments with three or four other attorneys to determine the ballpark charge for your kind of case. If the lawyer is way out of line, you might want to avoid him. If, on the other hand, he charges top dollar, it might be because he's that good. Your willingness to pay more money should depend on the urgency of your matter and the ramifications if you lose. A bankruptcy, an uncontested divorce, and the drawing up of a will are fairly simple and straightforward matters, and you should think twice about hiring an attorney who is asking for twice the going rate. If you have a DUI, however, and know of an attorney with a no-conviction record for drunk driving cases, you might feel he is entitled to extra compensation to guarantee you have the best representation.

Some other financial questions: How often will you receive bills? How frequently does the lawyer expect payment? What extras will you be paying for? Secretarial overtime? Faxing? Copying? What kind of hourly increments does the lawyer charge for phone calls? Don't underestimate these costs—they add up, as we've seen.

If it's on contingency, what will be the lawyer's percentage? What will fall under the category of "expenses," and do they come off the top before the pot is divided? If you lose, who pays the expenses? *This is a vital question.* Just because a lawyer advertises "If I lose I get nothing" doesn't mean that he means it. Many a contingency case client has lost in court and received a bill for the lawyer's expenses.

*Remember:* Everything is negotiable—fees, fee structure, everything. You can, for example, ask the lawyer to take less up front with the possibility of getting more when the case is settled. Will he reduce his hourly fee and agree to a percentage of the win? Trying to structure your legal payments to suit your economic situation makes sense, and your attorney may be perfectly willing to work with you to do that.

5. *What is the estimated cost of your case?* Here again, the attorney will probably go slippery on you, but you can still try to elicit a *range*. Ask her what she estimates it will cost if the other side comes to terms quickly versus full-blown litigation. The answers may not be precise, but at least you have a clearer idea of what you are facing and will be able to jump off if it looks like the train is going to be a runaway.

6. *What does he want for a retainer and what does it cover?* Is it refundable? Most attorneys will take a certain amount of money up front, then subtract the amount of work they do each month from the retainer. If your case is settled before the retainer is used up, the remainder should be refunded to you. Some will bill you each month as they use up the retainer to bring the amount back up to the original retainer. This is not an uncommon practice, and not unethical. It insures that the lawyer has a guarantee that you will pay your bill next month. Again, however, the amount not used up should be refunded to you at the end of your case. If the lawyer's contract stipulates that the retainer is nonrefundable, get another lawyer.

Another determination you must make is whether the

retainer the lawyer is asking for is too big. That can be roughly determined by gauging the answers to your other questions, namely, approximately how long your case will take to settle, how many hours the lawyer expects to work on it, and how much he charges per hour. If he estimates your matter will cost $5,000, and he wants a $2,500 retainer, the retainer is out of line. A more reasonable amount would be $1,000. There is no need to pay a lawyer in advance for a job he hasn't done yet, any more than you would pay a television repairman in advance to fix your set.

7. *Has the attorney had any experience dealing with the opposing side or the opposing side's counsel?* If so, what is their relationship? Are they friends? Enemies? Are there any factors that might constitute a conflict of interest, thus preventing your lawyer from serving you to the best of his ability? What is his win–loss ratio going up against the competition? Remember, an attorney can be too inflexible or too conciliatory in a dispute, depending on his frame of mind.

8. *Will the attorney provide a written contract spelling out the terms of your agreement?* Many states require attorneys to provide clients with written contracts unless the client specifically waives the right. *Don't waive your right.* Get it all down in black and white. If you don't, you will be getting what you deserve. If a lawyer tries to give you a runaround when you ask for a contract, find another lawyer. (Appendix A is a sample contract provided by a reputable business attorney.)

Don't be bashful in asking any of these questions, including if the attorney has ever been sued for malpractice. You are going to be shelling out big bucks, and you deserve the answers. If the attorney is honest and professional, he will not hesitate to answer them. In fact, he will probably be impressed by your intelligence and caution and will be more reluctant to try to cash in on your naïveté by padding your bills.

*Beware of:*

- The lawyer who tries to interpose a business judgment instead of legal advice. For instance, if you have a real estate transaction and the lawyer tells you you're paying too much for the property or the duration of the lease you are considering signing is too long, don't hire him. There are some exceptions, of course. If a person is inept in business, a widow, or an orphan, it would not be not wrong for an attorney to make sure his client is not being taken advantage of. *But you are not hiring a personal adviser or someone to tell you what to do with your life; you are only there for legal advice.* Your lawyer's only duty is to advise you of the legal risks involved in a deal; it's your call whether to take those risks. The cold fact is that most lawyers have no business experience outside their own offices, and few are good businesspeople.

- The attorney who immediately starts talking in legal gobbledygook and swamping you with unsolicited facts about the machinations of the legal process. The man is trying either to dazzle you with his knowledge of the law or to cover up his lack thereof. You won't be able to judge which until you get further down the road, and that could turn out to be a costly mistake. The law is ridiculously complicated enough without having your own lawyer add to the confusion. Your lawyer should communicate in a forthright, simple, understandable manner so that you can be aware of what is going on in your case at all times and make decisions based on that information.

- The specialist attorney who immediately refers you to another lawyer. It is common procedure for a lawyer who practices general law to refer a client to a specialist, just as doctors who are general practitioners refer patients to cardiologists. But when the attorney advertises himself to be a specialist and refers you to another specialist, it usually means that the case is too complicated for him or that it will require litigation and he has never been to court. This is most common among personal injury attorneys who like to settle cases in bulk. In many cases, these attorneys get paid for the referral, sometimes up to one-third of the fees the other attorney eventually collects. I have known attorneys who actually make a living passing off clients to other attorneys!

Because of widespread abuses and accusations of malpractice among lawyers who profit from referrals, some state bar associations have declared taking money for referrals illegal unless the referring attorney continues to work on the case. But because the bars' ethics rules don't stipulate what amount of work has to be done by the referring attorney to make him eligible to collect fees, lawyers skirt the rule by writing an occasional memo, summarizing a report, and writing meaningless letters to the second attorney.

If an attorney is unwilling or not competent enough to take your case, forget his referral and resume your own search. Good attorneys don't associate with or take referrals from *schlock* attorneys.

- The attorney who allows your interview to be interrupted by telephone calls, whose desk is littered with papers, and who seems distracted. Your problem is important to you. That is why you are there. If the lawyer can't even pretend for half an hour that it is important to him, too, it probably isn't.

- The overly aggressive attorney who tries to sell himself too hard. This type of lawyer is the used car salesman who tells you that you'd better snatch up that Ford because it will be gone tomorrow. You won't have to ask him about his victories with your type of case; he will unabashedly brag about them without your solicitation. At the same time, he will probably be sure to warn you of the dire consequences of your losing your case by having the "wrong kind" of representation. He might try to shove a retainer agreement in front of you and hand you a pen. If he does, tell him you would like to think about it and you'll call him back.

## Have a Backup Ready

In your quest for an attorney, you should have compiled a list of at least three or four names. After you've made your initial choice, keep the other names handy in case you become dissatisfied with your first choice's performance. Choosing a lawyer is like buying a used car; you won't know if it's okay until you drive it awhile. If you find you have a lemon, you might want to trade it in for another model before it costs you a lot of money for repairs.

# 6 Keeping the Costs Down

## Pre-Meeting Planning

The first thing you must determine before the first meeting with an attorney is what you are trying to accomplish. If you are trying to sell your business, for example, what is the bottom line you will accept after your legal fees are paid? If you are going through a divorce, what settlement in the way of alimony and child support will you take without going through a prolonged legal battle? If you are being charged with a crime, such as driving under the influence, do you want to go to trial to achieve an acquittal or do you want to arrange a plea bargain? If you prefer the latter, what kind of punishment will you be willing to live with?

In making this assessment, it is crucial that you view your problem with *objective detachment*. Ego is your enemy. In any dispute, it is natural for the participants to become emotionally involved. None of us likes to swallow the bitter pill of defeat.

None of us wants to be taken advantage of. None of us wants to appear to be backing down. But there are different degrees of losing, just as there are different degrees of winning. You can win the battle but lose your entire army in the process.

Once you make a rational assessment of your goal, use that goal to make a list of the points you won't concede and the ones that you don't care so much about. That way, you will be able to make clear to your attorney what your objectives are, saving his time and your money.

Defining your goal and what you want your lawyer to accomplish will largely depend on your finances. What kind of shape are they in and how well will they hold up when under attack by your attorney? If you have a cash flow problem today, but are expecting some money later, you might want to try to set up your payment plan accordingly.

Before your initial meeting, write down the history of your case in detail. If the first meeting is not free, send a copy of your history to the lawyer in advance so that he will be acquainted with your case before you get there. The letter should be concise (not more than five or six pages) and businesslike and should describe only the salient details of the problem. Avoid emotional references to the bad character of the opposition.

Even if the attorney has not read what you've sent him by the time of your first meeting, such a history will not only clarify for yourself the nature of your legal problem and the sequence of events that led up to it, it will also give the lawyer a convenient reference so that he won't have to call you up fourteen times and ask questions at $200 an hour. It will also help him save time in composing any correspondence to opposing counsel.

## Billing

Lawyers will bill whatever they can get away with. The trick is not letting them get away with it.

As we have said, determine what method of billing would be best for you. If you have a temporary cash flow problem, explain it to the lawyer and try to arrange for payment later (this is not all that uncommon).

If you have a very complicated legal case that looks as if it might drag on for a long time, ask the lawyer if he or she will accept a cap on fees. One caveat: When an attorney agrees to a cap, the cap will invariably be more than his estimated costs. The fee cap is *not* a way to cut your legal bills in half, but is merely an insurance policy against a worst-case scenario. Say, for example, the attorney estimates that the legal bills for your case will be between $30,000, if there is an out-of-court settlement, and $60,000, if it goes to full-blown litigation. The lawyer might be willing to cap his fees at $75,000, which is considerably more than his highest estimate, but considerably less than a possible bill of $120,000 in the event of complications.

Whether a lawyer will agree to cap his fees will depend on how hungry the attorney is for your business and the degree of faith he has in his own estimates. If a lawyer exhibits a lack of confidence in his ability to estimate your legal costs, it could indicate that he doesn't have much faith in other things he has told you or in other aspects of his professional abilities.

Even if you can't pay a lot of money up front or are dependent on the lawyer settling your case before he can get paid, ask for *itemized* statements reflecting the amount and nature of the work done. If the lawyer lists "Letter to Opposing Counsel re: strike motion—4 hours," take a look at the attorney's letter written on that date. Unless it is a lengthy and complex communication, you have a right to question the fee. Anyone can write a routine letter in less than four hours unless he is incompetent.

Ask to be billed *monthly*, even if your arrangement for payment is on some other basis. You must keep track of how the lawyer is spending your money, and how fast, so that you can maintain control of the situation. Too many people remain willfully ignorant of what kind of legal bills they are amassing until it is too late. (A sample of what your itemized legal bill should look like is in Appendix C.)

If you have questions about certain items on your statement, *bring them up as they arise.* It won't do you any good to complain after you've paid the tab. For instance, if you are dealing with a large law firm and you see an item on your bill for an outrageous sum to draft a simple motion, find out who did the drafting. If your attorney assigned the task to a novice associate just out of law school (this is not atypical), you are getting the shaft and have a right to complain. You didn't agree to pay big bucks to be part of the firm's training program.

Similarly, if your lawyer works for a large or medium-sized law firm and your bill includes numerous entries for in-house consultations, either your lawyer is padding the bill by spreading your wealth around the office or he doesn't know his job. If, on the other hand, your legal matter is very complex, it may be that the attorney legitimately needs to consult someone at the firm who is an expert on that type of matter. If that's the case, find out who that person is and try to hire *him.*

As previously noted, depositions can be very expensive. Many lawyers take an extraordinary number of depos not just to generate income, but out of the fear of a malpractice suit. Tell your lawyer upfront that you would like to be advised who is going to be deposed, what is expected to be learned, and how many lawyers will be in attendance during the depositions.

If you find out after the fact that your bill includes heavy costs for depositions, ask your attorney the same questions. Find out what the lawyer learned from the various witnesses. If the lawyer's reasons for deposing a witness are weak, that is, if the witness has little or nothing to do with your case, ask your lawyer to justify the expense.

Also ask to see the depositions. If they were done by a firm that used eight characters per inch instead of twelve or oversized margins, point that out to your attorney. More than likely, the attorney will tell you that he uses a certain deposition service because he can be assured of the quality of its work. That may be true. Then again, there may be other reasons.

Get the name of the deposition service. Call it and ask if it gives 10 percent discounts to attorneys who pay their bills within ten days. If so, and your attorney received the discount, ask that the savings be passed along to you.

Letting your lawyer know you are not a pushover and are carefully reviewing the bills he sends you will put him on notice and will make him wary of billing you indiscriminately.

Although we earlier criticized the new trend in "value billing," there might be an instance in which it could work to your advantage. Once you get the lawyer's best- and worst-case fee scenarios, he might be amenable to accepting an incentive arrangement whereby he would be rewarded for getting the job done expeditiously and economically. The lawyer might agree to work on an hourly basis plus a bonus if he finishes the job under a certain amount. For instance, say the lawyer estimates the costs of your case will be between $5,000 and $25,000. You might strike an arrangement whereby if he gets your job done in a satisfactory manner for $7,000, he will receive an extra $2,500, giving him an incentive to get the job done faster.

Remember: The main incentive under which lawyers operate is to drag things out as long as they can to drive up their costs. Any way you can hedge against that will be in your favor.

### Ask for Copies of Everything

Tell your lawyer you want copies of all correspondence, pleadings, and documents he sends out on your behalf. If the lawyer's efforts are to end in the production of a contract, ask for copies of the various drafts. As lawyers review a draft of an agreement, they will determine that certain changes should be made, in which event it is customary to underline the proposed changes so that each party need not reread the entire document as it goes through revision. This is known as the "redline" process.

It is important to review all "redline" copies for several reasons. One, you can see whether you are being billed big bucks for minor changes. Two, it will give you insight into how your attorney is conducting your case. For instance, your attorney may assure you that he is acting in a reasonable and accommodating manner and the other side is being un-cooperative and out of line, when in reality it may be the other way around. If your lawyer keeps inserting language into a contract that is unacceptable to the other side, it may be that he is just trying to keep the legal meter running.

This may sound elementary, but read *every word* of any document your lawyer sends you, then *read it again*. Don't assume that just because your lawyer has a law degree that he won't make a mistake in language or poorly word a document. Mistakes that can prove to be very costly later may be avoided by careful reading.

### Keep Track of Time

Every time you visit the lawyer in his office will cost you money. How much money depends on how much of his time you take up. Therefore, it is in your interest to take up as little as possible.

Arrive for meetings prepared. Outline beforehand the points you want to make and make them in a businesslike manner. If the lawyer starts to talk about the weather or the current baseball strike, politely cut him off.

Keep a diary. After you leave the attorney's office, note the time and make a note of it later, along with what was discussed and any directions you gave him. When you receive your monthly statement, check it against your records just to make sure you are not being billed for phantom time.

The same goes for any telephone conversations you have with the attorney. Most attorneys bill a minimum amount for a phone call—for example, two-tenths of an hour—even if they talked to you for a minute and a half. That doesn't mean you have to stand for it. The lawyer will probably argue that he can't be expected to time every call. But somehow all lawyers miraculously know when you go over your two-tenths-of-an-hour increment into the next twelve minutes. Demand you be billed accurately for phone time. You may not win on this point, but it will be ammunition for you later when you argue about how much you are being charged. Again, make sure you write down what was discussed. A lot of attorneys will call you up on a pretext that has little to do with your case, just to run up the bill. Don't stand for it.

Consider whether mailing the attorney a note or sending a fax may be more economical than communicating by phone. Perhaps a secretary can answer your question. If so, check your bill to make sure you don't end up paying for the lawyer's time.

## The Contract

The first rule of thumb in dealing with an attorney's contract or "fee agreement" is to read it carefully. If an attorney hands you a contract during your initial visit and asks you to sign on the dotted line, tell him you'd like to take it home and go over it at your leisure. If he tells you that it's just a "standard agreement," tell him you'd still like to read it at home.

There is really no such thing as a standard agreement, but there are some things that should be in every attorney's contract that you should insist on.

*Scope of Services.* This paragraph should say in rough form what the lawyer will be doing for you. It should mention specifically what the nature of your legal problem is and how the attorney will be expected to represent you. If the contract is a fill-in-the-blanks kind, your specific legal matter should be described at least in simplified form in a side letter.

*Duties of Attorney and Client.* The attorney should commit in writing to keep the client informed of significant legal developments and to respond to the client's inquiries in a timely manner. The client should agree to keep the attorney informed and to tell the attorney the truth.

*Billing Rates.* This section should lay out what the attorney charges, as well as what he bills for associate attorneys, paralegals, and secretaries. In a criminal case, the contract should specify what the charges will be for specific types of legal procedures, such as preliminary hearings, trials and motions, or motor vehicle hearings.

*Expenses.* The client is usually obliged to pay for all "reasonable" expenses incurred by the attorney. What is reasonable to an attorney, however, may not be reasonable to you. You should discuss with the attorney up front exactly what he charges for so it doesn't come as a shock later.

*Statements and Billing Periods.* This section should describe how often the lawyer will bill you and how often he expects to be paid. If you have special financial circumstances, like a cash flow problem, and the attorney has agreed verbally to work with you, such as arranging to delay payments, he should have no problem working this into the contract language, or at least referencing it in a side letter.

*Discharge or Withdrawal.* The client should be able to discharge the attorney at any time for any reason. The attorney, on the other hand, should be able to withdraw only for "good cause," namely, a client breach. Such a breach may be the client refusing to cooperate with the attorney, the client refusing to follow the attorney's advice on a material matter, or any circumstance that would render the attorney's continued representation unlawful or unethical.

*Retainer.* This paragraph should spell out how much the client has given the attorney as a retainer and how that retainer applies toward the lawyer's fees and costs. It should be specified in the contract that unused portions of the retainer should be refunded to the client at the conclusion of the client's case.

Some lawyers try to keep the retainer no matter how little of it is used up settling a client's legal problems. Don't let them. You wouldn't think of paying admission to eat in a restaurant, would you?

Determine what happens to the balance of the retainer if the attorney is discharged. Often attorneys slip a proviso into their contracts that they keep the entire retainer if they get fired. Don't go for it.

*Insurance.* It should be specified in the contract that the attorney have malpractice and/or liability insurance. The law in some states requires that lawyers carry such insurance. Your attorney should carry the minimum amount required or, better yet, an amount in excess of the law. If the attorney botches your case and ruins your life, you want to be able to collect damages when you sue.

(A sample contract acquired from a reputable attorney is in Appendix A.)

### Stay Involved With Your Case

This is absolutely vital. The number-one mistake a client can make is to ignore his or her own case. The client who tells his attorney, "Take care of this matter and call me when it's over," is asking to be taken to the cleaners. This is not to say that you should call your lawyer every day and ask for an update on your case. That is, not unless you want him to own your house.

One important aspect of staying involved is being aware of

important deadlines in your case. For instance, for every type of lawsuit there is a statute of limitations within which the case must be filed. In California, personal injury suits must be filed within a year of an accident. In bankruptcy and probate cases, certain filings have to be made within time frames specified by law. If a lawsuit is filed against you, your attorney must file an answer denying your culpability. In most states, that period of time is thirty days, although it can be extended for various reasons. Once an answer is filed, the case is "at issue," and an "at issue memorandum" must be filed with the court before a trial date can be set. If these and other filings are not made in a timely manner, it can result in a dismissal of the case by the courts. *Probably more lawsuits have been botched by attorneys' failing to make timely and proper filings than for any other reason.*

Ask your attorney for a timeline for your case. By which date must the case be filed? What are the essential filings the lawyer must make in your case and when must they be made according to law? What other legal steps does the lawyer intend to take as the case progresses, such as pretrial motions, settlement conferences, preliminary hearings, actual trial dates, etc., and when does he anticipate those steps will be taken?

Make a list of these dates and *make sure the lawyer is sticking to his own timetable.* As a deadline approaches, call your attorney to make sure he is aware of it or has already met it. If the lawyer tells you he has made the filing with the court, ask him for a copy of the document stamped by the court clerk. If he hems and haws at your request, it might behoove you to check with the court clerk to verify that your lawyer is telling you the truth. If you find your attorney is lying to you, get another attorney immediately. If your attorney admits he has not filed the proper papers yet, but tells you not to worry, he will get it done, take a look at your own timeline. If he has had six months to file suit and the deadline is up in a week, it might not be advisable to wait five days to find yourself another lawyer.

If there is going to be a delay in your case, ask your attorney why. If he tries to brush you aside with a platitude like, "There's a scheduling conflict," ask to be informed exactly what that means. If it translates to "benefit dinner" or "golf game," put your foot down. If your lawyer is willing to sacrifice your legal interests for his own recreation, he may not be the best man to handle your case in court.

Ask your attorney not only for a timeline, but for an estimated cost of each segment of the timeline. For instance, if your case involves litigation, ask for an estimate of legal fees for the various stages of the litigation, such as pretrial hearings or motions and demurrers. This will help you get an idea of whether your legal costs are escalating out of sight and whether it might be advisable to settle instead of fight.

One method you might employ to aid you in this process is "decision-tree analysis." In business, this method of analysis is often used in conditions of uncertainty to compute the likelihood of various outcomes. Decisions are viewed as branches of a tree, and as one proceeds along each branch, certain expectations are computed.

At each critical juncture of your timeline, say, the first set of pretrial motions, ask your attorney to guess your chances of success. Are they 30 percent or 60 percent? What happens if the motions are successful? If the judge denies the motions, how long will it take you to get to trial? What are the chances of success if you go to trial? If you lose at trial, what are the chances of winning on appeal? At any point, you can weigh your percentages and make your decision to proceed or settle accordingly.

### Watch for Overlawyering

If a lawyer produces a ninety-page document when a twelve-page document is sufficient, he's padding the bill.

Many lawyers will try to tell you that by doing so, they are protecting your interests. Lawyers like to spout off doomsday scenarios; it helps them justify being slow, deliberate, and sickeningly fastidious. But remember, prophets have been predicting the end of the world for thousands of years. If your lawyer tries to tell you about doomsday, analyze the likelihood of it and make your decisions on that basis.

This is not to say ignore his or her advice. Lawyers deal with problems; that's their business. They have seen lots of things go wrong, and their job is to help you avoid such eventualities. However, there can come a point in any negotiation in which the bargaining process can break down through overlawyering. At that point, you must make your own decision and rein in your attorney.

For example, if your attorney issues dire warnings and spins a scenario of possible disaster, ask him if he's personally seen such a situation occur and under what circumstances. Also ask him *how often* he has seen it happen. If he has negotiated a hundred deals and his doomsday scenario has only happened once, you might want to ask yourself if guarding against it is worth throwing the entire deal into jeopardy.

Which leads to another point: Overlawyering can not only be costly, it can ultimately kill a deal and thereby defeat the purpose of hiring the lawyer in the first place. We have been involved in many contract negotiations in which the attorney for one side, in an attempt to predict and forestall any and all scenarios which would have a negative effect on his client, created an atmosphere of distrust between the negotiating parties and produced a document so untenably one-sided that it led to the other party walking away from the deal.

A friend of ours recently experienced this when he hired a law firm to draft a prenuptial agreement. The client informed the attorneys that his fiancée was not very happy about signing such an agreement, but that she would do so provided it was restricted to certain key assets that the client wished to protect. The client instructed the attorneys to draw up the agreement on that basis, but when the document was finished, the attorneys had itemized every asset the client owned. The agreement infuriated the fiancée, who then hired her own attorney. The end result was that in order for our friend to shield the assets he wanted shielded, he had to agree to give away rights on a lot of other assets that would have normally been protected even if he hadn't had a prenuptial. A few years later, when he got divorced, he discovered he would have fared better without the agreement.

What many people don't realize is that there is an *incentive* on the part of many attorneys to kill deals. If a deal is made and it goes sour later on, the attorney does not want to take the blame. It is safer for him to nitpick the agreement to death up front in the guise of protecting his client's interests. The lawyer still gets his money if the deal goes sour, but can then point to the other side and say, "See, he was intending to screw you. Otherwise, he would have been willing to sign."

What attorneys fail to realize is that in negotiating any deal, *you have to look at who is sitting across the table from you*. Predicting disaster from the outset sets a tone of mistrust and can often create a feeling of ill-will between parties. If you sit down to work out a business agreement and the other side's attorney starts out by assuming you are a thief, more than likely you will feel insulted. It is important to stay on top of your attorney during the negotiations and rein him in if he starts getting out of hand. You probably have a better feel for whom you're dealing with than he does.

One way to tell if a lawyer has a tendency to overlawyer is to look at the number of adjectives he uses if a lawsuit has to be filed because the other party did not live up to the terms of an agreement. For instance, if you see a paragraph in which the lawyer claims the defendant "wantonly, wrongfully, maliciously, with full knowledge and intent, without reasonable justification, did breach, violate, and contravene the intent of said agreement," you know you have an overlawyer on your hands. All that previous statement says is that someone violated the terms of an agreement. The only reason for the extra verbiage is that the client is paying for every word.

### Reducing the Lawyer's Workload

You know the facts that led up to your legal situation better than anyone, including your lawyer. While he might have to hire an investigator (very expensive) to track down witnesses or research documents, you might be able to do these things yourself and save yourself a considerable sum in the process. This is not to say you should be *interviewing* witnesses or playing private eye. There is an art to getting information out of people that a trained investigator will know that you probably won't. You might just end up irritating your lawyer and damaging your own case rather than helping it. On the other hand, you may be able to acquire information easily that your lawyer or any investigator assigned to your case would have to hunt down.

For instance, if your lawyer is going to need financial records, check records, invoices, papers of incorporation, or business correspondence, you can assemble a package of what you think he might need. Take some time and organize it in chronological order so the lawyer can get a sense of how your case developed over time. Since your legal problem started before your attorney got involved, you have a better grasp of who the significant players are. Make a list of them, along with their addresses and telephone numbers and what roles they played in your case. If the case is likely to involve litigation, jot down whether you think witnesses will be sympathetic or hostile.

Remember: If an investigator's fingers do the walking, it could end up costing you $100 an hour. If you can save him some time by putting in some of your own, you'll be ahead of the game.

## Auditing Firms

An increasing number of accounting and consulting firms—as well as some law firms themselves—have begun offering clients auditing services in order to help them decipher their legal bills and ferret out overcharges.

Once retained, the auditing firm will typically run the legal bills in question through a custom computer system to red-flag questionable items. After that, one of the firm's auditors or lawyers goes through every time sheet, every motion, every memo, then produces a report quantifying discrepancies between work done and work charged for and recommending itemized reductions. In addition, the client will often get recommendations for improving case management and sometimes recommendations for alternative billing methods. In some cases, the firms offer expert witness testimony in case you decide to sue your lawyer or will intervene with the attorney for you in an effort to get your bill reduced.

The billing methods these auditing firms use vary. Many, like Bala Cynwyd, Pennsylvania–based Legalgard, Inc., or Encino, California's Legal Cost Control Consultants (LC3), charge the client a percentage of what they identify in the way of overcharges. For instance, in one of its ads, LC3 identifies overcharges of $75,000 on a legal bill of $375,000, at a cost to the client of $5,500, for a net savings of $69,500.

Some other firms, like Stuart, Maue, Mitchell and James, Ltd., of St. Louis, charge a flat fee based on a legal bill's size and complexity. Most of the bills Stuart, Maue, Mitchell and James looks at are in the $250,000 range and an audit can cost the client up to $20,000.

The drawbacks to utilizing such a firm's services are obvious. Because they deal in percentages, most auditing firms will not take on small clients, but will deal only with bills of six figures and higher. And even if you do have such whopping legal costs, such firms don't charge you a percentage of what they recover for you from your lawyer, but of what they identify as overcharges. Thus, an audit may result in additional costs if your attorney declines to refund you any money.

In the end, what such firms offer is not guaranteed savings, but leverage to use against your lawyer to make him more reasonable or ammunition to use against him if you decide to sue.

### Arbitration

If you feel your lawyer has overbilled you and you cannot resolve the problem by talking, and you don't want to go to the expense of hiring another lawyer and filing a lawsuit, you can go to your local bar association and request fee arbitration. Arbitration is an out-of-court hearing during which one or more disinterested parties will listen to both sides, weigh the evidence, and decide whether the fees charged are proper.

In most instances, the lawyer must submit to arbitration, even if he or she has sued you for the money and even if you and the lawyer have a written fee agreement. (One exception is if the lawyer has sued you in small claims court before the arbitration proceeding was begun.)

Most county and city bar associations offer arbitration services at a nominal fee ($10 to $100), but if your local bar does not have an arbitration program or you think the local program will not give you a fair hearing, you can contact your state bar and ask if it has a mandatory fee arbitration office.

The forms you will need to file for arbitration will ask you the type of case (divorce, personal injury, etc.), the amount the lawyer charged you as well as the amount you are disputing, and whether you wish the arbitration to be *binding* or *nonbinding*. Binding arbitration is final, without possibility of appeal, whereas in nonbinding arbitration either you or the attorney can ask for a civil trial if one of you is not satisfied with the outcome.

One important point: If you have not paid your lawyer and he or she is planning to sue you for the money, you might receive notification from the attorney of your right to arbitrate. In many jurisdictions, you must file your arbitration request and forms with your local bar within a specified period of time (usually thirty days) after you receive the notification. Otherwise your right to arbitration may terminate.

# 7 Firing Your Attorney

Firing your attorney can be a tricky business, full of pitfalls for the unwary client.

Clients are often reluctant to replace their attorneys for any number of good reasons. Maybe they have already paid the lawyer a considerable sum and are afraid of losing their investment; they are in the middle of a legal process which they find intimidating and bewildering and fear losing their legal guide; they are closing in on an important court date and finding new counsel at the eleventh hour is not an option; they are disenchanted with the first lawyer, and so believe that the next one will be just as bad.

The key is to determine early in the game whether your attorney is dishonest, stupid, inept, or lazy or is beset by personal problems (marital, health, addiction) that will endanger the outcome of your case. That way, you can dump him or her and have enough time to bring another lawyer on board.

## Early Warning Signs

1. *The lawyer doesn't return your phone calls.*

This is one sure sign you should get someone else on board *immediately*. Occasionally, an attorney will be out of his office for extended periods of time, especially if he or she is in court trying a case. But there is absolutely no excuse for any attorney not to return your call within a reasonable period of time. If your lawyer doesn't call you back, it's because (a) he doesn't want to tell you that he's done nothing; (b) he has done something that has harmed your case; or (c) because of personal or other problems, he doesn't care about your case. It never ceases to amaze us when we hear of clients who have gone *years* without getting a phone call back from their attorneys and had their cases dismissed because the statute of limitations ran out on them. If your lawyer doesn't return your phone calls within forty-eight hours, dump him.

2. *There are delays in your case and the attorney is evasive when you ask him why.*

Watch out for such platitudes as "These things take time" or "The wheels of justice grind slowly." If he cites "scheduling conflicts," demand to know exactly what the conflicts are.

3. *The attorney is always working up to a deadline.*

Study your case timeline and get to know exactly when the first deadlines come up. Check with the attorney to make sure he has performed the timely task he was supposed to. *Don't just take the attorney's word for it.* Ask to see the documentation stamped by the court clerk.

Missed deadlines are perhaps the most common crime of inept and lazy attorneys and the biggest danger to a client's case. If the attorney stalls about providing you with the documentation you request, take a trip down to the court-house and check out the clerk's records. Expending the effort early enough to find out that your lawyer is a flake could turn out to be the best investment you could make.

If your attorney procrastinates with you, he probably procrastinates with the rest of his clients. If you repeatedly call his office to talk to him and his secretary tells you the lawyer is too busy to talk or that he has a deadline to meet, take it as a sign. If his secretary calls you up and tells you that you have to get over to the office immediately to sign a document, you can be sure the lawyer's working against a deadline.

Beware of the lawyer who wants you to sign verification sheets in blank. These papers are printed forms attached to various affidavits and pleadings signed under oath and under penalty of perjury. Some lawyers will get these papers signed in advance so they can work on their own deadline time frame without having to go to all the trouble to contact the client. If your lawyer tries this, refuse, then find someone else.

4. *The lawyer seems uninterested in your case.*

During meetings, he acts distracted, allows your meeting to be interrupted by phone calls, shuffles papers, and gives you and your case halfhearted attention. Dump him. You need someone to devote his full time to your problem; that's what you're paying for.

Corollary: The lawyer tries to turn you over to an underling associate at the firm. If you hired Saul, demand Saul. If Saul doesn't think you're important enough to warrant his attention, find someone who does.

5. *The lawyer has a substance abuse problem.*

This may be harder to detect, but take note of any erratic behavior the lawyer exhibits, such as extreme restlessness, inattention, hyperactivity, or slurred speech. We are not being facetious with this warning. Because of the stressful nature of the work and widespread dissatisfaction within the legal profession, alcohol and drug abuse among lawyers is significantly higher than in the population at large. It is estimated that 18 percent of all lawyers are heavy drinkers, compared to 10 percent of the rest of the population. If your meeting is in the afternoon and your attorney smells of booze, he may have just had a martini at lunch. Still, consider it a warning. If you meet with him *before* lunch and you smell alcohol, start shopping elsewhere.

6. *The attorney has an attitude problem.*

This can be exhibited in many ways. The attorney may act arrogant and condescending. He may be consumed by his own ego and constantly brag about his courtroom successes. He may be overly aggressive. He may refuse to do what you tell him to or argue with you about a business point, telling you that his judgment is better than your own. *You are the boss; the attorney is the paid help.* It is absolutely vital that the attorney understand that. If he doesn't, find one who does.

7. *The first bill from the attorney is a whopper and very little work has been done.*

Sit down with the lawyer and ask for an explanation of how the simple tasks listed on the bill could take so long. If he answers with evasive platitudes or convoluted legalese or if he high-handedly refuses to justify the cost of tasks on the bill, you should probably shop elsewhere. If you go along and swallow his line at this point, he will know he's got you, guaranteeing that the bills won't get any smaller as your case progresses.

8. *You find out your lawyer* isn't.

Don't laugh; this is not as farfetched as it sounds. Every year, fake lawyers are exposed throughout the country. Many of these people have been paralegals or have worked in law offices and thus know the ins and outs and the jargon of the profession. The *New York Times* recently reported the case of Steven Welchons, who practiced in Madison County, New York, as a public defender for years, representing over a thousand clients. He was only found out when one of them complained. Welchons, who had never even graduated from college, even succeeded in fooling his wife.

If you suspect that your lawyer's credentials are bogus, call your state bar and ask for the membership records department. If your lawyer is not registered as a licensed member of the bar, ask for a referral to the proper law enforcement agency and report him.

## Not-So-Early Warning Signs

Sometimes, after expending a lot of time and a large amount of money on legal bills, a client—particularly the client who doesn't stay abreast of his own case, naively thinking that his attorney is handling everything for him—finds that his blind trust has been misplaced. Hopefully, the awakening comes at a point where something can be salvaged from the disaster.

1. *The attorney is selling out your interests*. This most often happens when:

a. The lawyer views his relationship with the other side's counsel as more important than your relationship with him.

b. The attorney sees his business relationship with the other attorney's client as more important than his relationship with you. (Entertainment attorneys, for example, want to stay on good terms with the major studios which provide them with most of their business; therefore, an individual client's interests can be subverted in negotiations. Similarly, lawyers who do a lot of business with insurance companies may be more interested in preserving their relationship with the insurer than in looking out for their own clients.)

c. The attorney has a blatant conflict of interest he's not telling you about, like representing two clients from the same auto accident. (This does happen.)

d. The lawyer is incompetent, is afraid of litigation, or has a cash flow problem, and pushes you to accept a smaller settlement than your case merits.

e. The lawyer doesn't like to try cases and makes his money by referring his clients to colleagues for a fee.

f. The attorney doesn't like you, considers you a nuisance, and wants to get rid of you.

2. *In the middle of your case, your attorney wants to renegotiate his fee without good reason.*

This is a strategy used by unscrupulous attorneys, especially when they know they have their clients over a barrel. It is often used close to an impending deadline.

We became aware of one particularly egregious instance of this a few years ago when a woman I knew was indicted for a major felony. On the eve of the pretrial, the attorney approached her and told her he needed more money or he would have to withdraw from the case. The woman had already paid attorney's fees in the six figures and had no more cash available. Terrified by the possibility of going to jail, she ended up signing over the deeds to two pieces of property. The case was dismissed in pretrial and the woman was so relieved by the outcome that she did nothing about the extortion.

Note that we said "tries" to renegotiate his fee *without good reason*. There are many cases which for reasons beyond the control of the attorney turn out to be much more complicated and time-consuming than the attorney at first anticipated. In such cases, particularly those in which a flat fee has been agreed upon, it is not necessarily unreasonable for an attorney to ask for a reevaluation of his fees. You wouldn't work for free. Don't expect your attorney to, either.

3. *The attorney is stealing from you.*

This happens most often when attorneys are handling trust account monies, such as in estate settlements or personal injury cases, or have the power of attorney to write checks for businesses or elderly people who have been found incompetent to handle their own affairs.

The big problem here is that in most cases, by the time the client finds out his lawyer is a thief, it is too late. Misappropriation of client funds is grounds for disbarment, but that is little consolation to you if your money is gone.

## How to Fire Your Attorney

1. If you feel your attorney is messing up, try to get together with him for a powwow. Explain to him your concerns. If the attorney dodges your calls or, when you do get together, is evasive or unresponsive, get rid of him. If he says, "You're right, I know I've messed up, but I'll do better," you have a judgment call to make. You either believe him or you don't.

2. If your decision is to replace Attorney A and you have no B in mind, try to locate one as quickly as possible, since A will bill you up to the last hour you retain him. If you do have B in mind, he will probably want to be sure that you have fired A before he will agree to represent you.

3. Fire your attorney in writing. A telephone call won't do it. If you're going to fire him, you probably won't be able to get him on the phone anyway.

State in the letter the reasons you are firing him, such as his not returning phone calls or refusing to respond to your letters. Don't go overboard in the letter. Do not discuss his ancestry or anything you cannot prove. You do not need to violate libel laws in order to retrieve your file. Simply request that he turn over your file to you or your new attorney immediately and a refund of the unused portion of your original retainer. Attorney A has a right to photocopy the file for his records, *without charge or cost to you*, but you are entitled to the original documents.

If you're on your own and you owe Attorney A some money beyond the amount you paid as a retainer, he might try to hold your file hostage for payment. A lawyer has no right to do this, but it is done frequently. This is another reason why it is critical not only to keep copies of everything you give your attorney, but to demand copies from him of everything he

does—every letter, every motion, etc.—as your case progresses. If possible, keep *original* documents yourself and give
your attorney photocopies.

Many attorneys will keep your retainer, even if they have
not used it all up. They can do this by sending you a padded
final bill to make up the difference or by just ignoring your
request for a refund. Even if you have considered this possibility and covered it in your original contract, the chances
are that you won't get the money back, so don't drive yourself
crazy over it. Once you hire Attorney B, you can request that
he write a demand letter to Attorney A for the return of your
funds, but remember, that letter will cost you money and is
not guaranteed to get you results. The best defense you have
is to try to keep the retainer as low as possible so that the loss
is relatively painless.

If you have signed a contingency fee contract, giving the
attorney a percentage of any recovery, he can file a lien with
the court and will be paid a reasonable amount for his
services rendered. This is called "quantum meruit."

Specify in the letter that if your file is not returned
promptly, a complaint will be filed with the state bar. Refusal
to return a client's file subjects the attorney to disciplinary
action and such a letter will usually bring results.

4. If a lawsuit has been filed on your behalf, it is necessary
to notify the court of your change in legal representation by
filing a "Substitution of Attorney" form. This relieves Attorney
A of further responsibility. If you have found Attorney B and
he has expressed a willingness to take your case, he can
handle this for you. If you have not yet retained Attorney B,
you can substitute yourself in pro per, which means that you
are representing yourself.

In most cases, once you have notified Attorney A that you
wish to change representation, he or she will provide the
Substitution of Attorney form and will file it with the court. It
is a good practice, however, to get a duplicate so that you can

file it yourself in case the original does not get filed. Check with the court clerk to make sure the change of attorney has been recorded.

If Attorney A is uncooperative or unreachable and you have no Attorney B yet, you can file your own substitution motion with the court.

If you have followed the advice in this book, you should have received by this time copies of various court documents labeled "Pleadings." The face sheet on these papers will have the name of the case, the file number, and the name of the court where the proceedings have been instituted. Though the format varies from state to state, the name of the lawyer, along with his address and telephone number, will ordinarily appear in the upper left-hand corner. Also, the legal papers generally have line numbers indented from the left margin. If you don't have copies of the pleadings, go to the court clerk's office in the courthouse and purchase at a minimal cost a photocopy of the face sheet and take down the names, addresses, and phone numbers of all other attorneys involved in the case. Ask the clerk for the department (sometimes called "division") where "law and motion" matters are heard. Also find out the days and times of day such matters are normally handled and how many days before the hearing you have to mail notice of the fact you want to dump your attorney.

Obtain appropriately numbered blank legal paper from a stationery store, together with a form entitled "Affidavit of Service." Type in the name of the court, the title of the case and its number, and the date and time of the hearing exactly as it appears on the face page, paying particular attention to the line numbers so as to duplicate the copy, with the exception that you will label it "Notice of Motion to Remove Counsel." Put your name, address, and telephone number where the lawyer's address appears on the copy. In the body of the page, insert: "To all parties concerned, take notice that _____ [you] will on the ____ day of ____, at the hour of ____,

in Department _____ of the above entitled court, move to relieve
_____ [lawyer's name] as the attorney for the undersigned
and substitute _____ [you] as attorney in pro per." The
motion will be supported by the affidavit attached. In the
affidavit, set forth your reasons for dismissing the attorney as
objectively and, concisely as possible.

Copies should be sent to all attorneys involved. Have
someone over the age of eighteen, who is not a party to the
case, sign and file the affidavit of mailing with the court,
along with the original (not duplicate pages). Chances are,
you will get your file without having to show up. The attorney
will in all likelihood consent to his/her removal. But if he has
a contingent fee agreement or you owe him/her any money,
expect him to file a lien against you.

## Firing the Client

You don't have to give your attorney a reason when you fire
him or her. You don't even have to have one. If your attorney,
on the other hand, wants to dump you as a client, he has to
tell you why.

Reasons a lawyer might want to get rid of a client are:

• The client has lied to the attorney.
• The client refuses to cooperate with the attorney.
• The client refuses to pay his bills.

The attorney-firing-client scenario would probably go
something like this:

The attorney calls you into the office and hands you your
file along with a request that you substitute yourself in pro
per. If you refuse, the attorney can make a motion with the
court stating his reasons why he no longer wants to represent
you. Unless you are in the middle of a trial, the motion will
usually be granted.

On rare occasions, the attorney seeking to get rid of you

and your case will ask you to sign a paper releasing him from all liability. *The lawyer cannot demand such a release, and if you do sign it, it is of no legal effect.* If the attorney puts such a release form in front of you, tell him you want to take it home and review it. Then fax it to the state bar, along with a letter explaining the circumstances.

## Filing a Complaint with the Bar

Lawyer disciplinary boards vary as to rules and procedures from state to state.

The medical profession provides a national listing of malpractice verdicts and disciplinary actions against doctors so that a doctor's reputation follows him from state to state. The legal profession, however, has been much more lenient on itself. The American Bar Association's National Discipline Data Bank lists only instances of public discipline, and the various state disciplinary boards are not required to deposit information into it. Since providing the information is voluntary for a state board and because such boards are notoriously understaffed and underfunded, the ABA data bank is grossly incomplete.

The fifty state disciplinary boards employ less than four hundred full-time lawyers, with four states—California, Texas, New York, and Pennsylvania—counting for 50 percent of those lawyers. With a few hundred lawyers trying to police 850,000, it is little wonder that a lot of lawyers are willing to push the ethical envelope. Add to that the fact that most state bar associations are secretive and uncommunicative, even with other state bar associations, and you have a fragmented system in which lawyers' peccadilloes all too frequently slip through the cracks. Even if a lawyer is found guilty of a felony and disbarred, it can be *years* before his name appears in the ABA data bank.

The American Bar Association Model Rules, which define

the ethical standards of the practice of law, provide a very fuzzy standard for lawyers to go by. Intentionally so. In 1983, the rules were rewritten and such words as "good," "right," "wrong," and "bad" were eliminated. In their places were substituted words like "prudent," "proper," "material," "permitted," and "substantial." With a stroke of a word processor, unethical behavior became merely equivocal. According to law professor Mary Anne Glendon, "The apparent explanation for deleting the Ethical Considerations is that once you get beyond such obvious no-nos as stealing clients' funds, consensus on what is right and wrong for lawyers is diminishing. In other words, the more moral confusion there is, the less guidance one should expect from formal codes of ethics."

Although the ABA Rules require a lawyer to report ethical violations by other lawyers, few do, even though they encounter them all the time. It's known as "professional courtesy."

While few lawyers snitch on their colleagues, many of them secretly enjoy it when the miscreants get caught. We know a lot of lawyers who subscribe to bar publications only for the disciplinary report section, to see who was suspended and disbarred and to chuckle at the accounts of incompetence and dishonesty in the profession. Unfortunately, the big laugh is at the expense of the poor clients who have suffered at the hands of their lawyers.

Still, reporting a lawyer's malfeasance or negligence to your local or state bar might be worth it. If the lawyer has had numerous other complaints filed against him, or if your grievance is serious enough, it could result in his or her being subjected to public reproval, probation, suspension, or disbarment. In any case, it can be psychologically satisfying to know you are putting the shaft to someone who shafted you.

Few if any bar associations have form complaints, primarily because there are so many legal specialties and so many ways that a client can be harmed that they would be impractical. So you will have to write a letter containing at least the following information:

1. Your name, address, and telephone number.

2. The name, address, and telephone number of the attorney you are reporting.

3. The type of legal matter involved, e.g., criminal, divorce, contract dispute, real estate, probate, etc.

4. The name of the case, the court in which it was filed, the case number, and the subject matter involved.

5. The date on which you retained the attorney and the amount of retainer and fees the attorney received.

6. What the attorney failed to do or did wrong and how it damaged you. State your case in detailed but not overly lengthy form, as objectively as possible, giving relevant dates. For example, did he miss a deadline, allowing the statute of limitations to expire? Did he fail to return your phone calls when you had valuable information to give him, resulting in your case being damaged? Did he ignore your requests for the return of your file after notice of dismissal? Did he fail to interview percipient witnesses? (In this case, you should attach statements of what the witnesses would have testified to if they had been subpoenaed.)

Don't waste your time writing a complaint letter just because you didn't like the verdict in your case or because you thought your attorney's performance in court was grossly inept. Incompetence of performance (unless specifically negligent) and "honest" mistakes are not grounds for censure. The bar, being composed of lawyers, *knows* most lawyers are inept. If they were censured for it, the professional ranks of lawyerdom would be decimated.

7. If you feel you were overcharged, state the amount and the services rendered.

Be forewarned that your complaint that your lawyer failed

to return the unused portion of your retainer will probably fall on deaf ears. Also, unless the amount overcharged is especially egregious, don't expect much sympathy here. Overcharging is a way of life for attorneys, including the lawyer on the disciplinary board reading your letter.

Keep in mind that your letter may result in little action, although writing it might make you feel better. But attorneys—particularly attorneys who are aware of their own gross incompetence and who tend to be repeat offenders—do fear censure by the bar. In such cases, an indication that you are considering reporting the attorney to the bar may get you more than would filing an actual complaint. At least you might get your file, and maybe even some money back.

If you get no action from the bar and you feel you have been seriously damaged by your attorney's actions or inaction, you can always look for another attorney and sue for malpractice.

## Filing a Malpractice Suit

Just a few years ago, legal malpractice suits were rare, as attorneys were reluctant to sue colleagues for fear of opening up a Pandora's box of internecine warfare in which their own competence would be challenged. But as medical malpractice suits emerged as a tremendously lucrative field of legal practice due to huge jury awards for damages, more and more attorneys cast off their code of "professional courtesy" and filed suits against their attorney brothers and sisters, to the point that nowadays eight out of every ten attorneys can be expected to be sued for malpractice at least once in their careers.

Many of these suits are not spawned by attorney incompetence or malfeasance. A majority are initiated by clients as cross-complaints after the lawyer has sued a client for non-payment of legal fees. "A lawyer who aggressively goes after a client for a big bill can elicit a cross-complaint for malpractice," says David Aleshire of the Orange County, California, law firm Rutan and Tucker. "That's why a lawyer has to keep a client current in paying his bills." Still, many cases are not only legitimate, but justified.

Malpractice lawsuits must involve a professional as a defendant, whether that be a doctor, an accountant, a lawyer, an engineer or any practitioner who holds himself out as being a member of a profession requiring a certain amount of experience and expertise. Second, the suit must allege that the professional did not perform certain acts or performed acts which did not comply with the standards of the profession.

Among grounds for a legal malpractice suit are:

1. Negligent acts or omissions (such as missing a deadline, failing to raise a proper defense, or not subpoenaing a vital witness) that result in the loss of the client's case or damage to the client. In this case, ignorance is no excuse for the attorney. It doesn't matter whether he inadvertently let a statute of limitations expire because he was involved in another case or whether he was unaware of the statutory deadline; he's *expected* to know about the deadline and meet it.

2. Going forward without the client's permission; for instance, an attorney gets a settlement offer and turns it down without the client's knowledge.

3. Excessive overbilling. (Here, only overcharged expenses can be recovered, but punitive damages can apply if the lawyer's conduct is egregious.)

4. Misrepresentation. (In his TV ads, the lawyer claims expertise in one or more areas of law when his experience is in reality limited or nonexistent.)

5. Theft of a client's funds.

If the attorney is not returning your calls and is generally unresponsive, the fear of a malpractice suit may not be a very efficient management tool. Just as a voodoo priest places a dead chicken on the doorstep of a person to let him *know* he's been cursed, drop the lawyer a letter and tell him you think he is committing malpractice.

Most lawyers *do* fear malpractice suits, however, which is why most carry malpractice insurance. And be assured that the cost of that insurance will be built into their rates and clients' bills. It is estimated that in the medical profession, 15 to 30 percent of the cost of medicine is attributable to defensive measures against malpractice suits, such as unnecessary precautionary testing. Although there is no way to gauge how much of a lawyer's costs are exacerbated by precautionary lawyering, there is no doubt that lawyers nowadays are going out of their way to create a written record to protect themselves. "You're definitely seeing lawyers writing memos to themselves and overdocumenting their files," says attorney David Baron of the Palm Springs, California, firm Slovak and Baron. "There's a lot of CYA going on and that is probably to some extent reflected in higher rates."

It seems here we have a vicious cycle. If most clients sue for malpractice because of the size of their bills and if the size of the lawyers' bills are being affected by lawyers' attempts to protect themselves from malpractice, clients will be more and more prone to sue, which is an incentive for lawyers to overlawyer more, which...

Rather than substituting one lawsuit for another, it would behoove you to carefully monitor your attorney's work so that you can determine early in the game whether your lawyer is incompetent. By the time you retain a malpractice attorney, you will in all likelihood have sustained serious damage, both financial and emotional, perhaps more than any malpractice judgment can rectify.

The key words again: STAY INVOLVED WITH YOUR CASE.

# PART III

## NAME YOUR GAME

# 8  Bankruptcy

During the late 1980s and the 1990s, as many U.S. industries downsized and underwent mass layoffs, millions of people, many for the first time in their lives, found themselves facing economic ruin. Bankruptcy suddenly became the legal specialty of choice.

Legal mills sprang up all over the country advertising bankruptcy as the panacea for the financial problems of the beleaguered public. "Call 1-800-NO-DEBTS and all your problems will be solved. Make your creditors go away. Bill collectors will stop calling you."

Because most Chapter 7 liquidation bankruptcies are routine and not tremendously time-consuming for an attorney, they can be relatively profitable, especially if the attorney can rope in a lot of clients. So don't believe that bankruptcy is the answer for you just because an attorney tells you so—especially one who advertises during the late movie. Which is just what Dr. Richard Bartowski* recently did, to his deep regret.

After undertaking an overly aggressive expansion of his lucrative Palm Springs, California, dental practice, Bartowski encountered financial problems. Although he was making a six-figure income, he found himself with a cash flow problem and a considerable amount of debt owed to building contractors and medical equipment suppliers. He looked in the yellow pages and found an attorney who advertised himself as a "bankruptcy specialist."

The attorney assured the concerned dentist that he had nothing to worry about, that he could buy Bartowski three years of time and stop any collection actions against him by filing Chapter 11 bankruptcy and reorganizing the dentist's business. Bartowski, impressed by the lawyer's confidence and his bedside manner, agreed to the plan and left the office relieved. He had no idea that the attorney ran a bankruptcy mill and was less concerned with the details of his clients' cases than with attracting a volume of business through advertising.

The one minor detail the attorney forgot in Dr. Bartowski's case was that to stay in business, the dentist needed drills, dental chairs, and other equipment, all of which were secured by a creditor who had loaned Bartowski a considerable sum of money.

The reorganization plan worked out by Bartowski's attorney was rejected by the court as inadequate and he was given a deadline to submit a new plan. In the meantime, the creditor made a motion to get a "relief from stay" (in short, he wanted his money), and when Bartowski's attorney failed to file a new reorganization plan on time, the court granted the motion.

The attorney was notified of the action by the court, but was so busy with his bankruptcy mill workload that he neglected to inform his client. Bartowski only learned about the developments when movers showed up at his office with a writ of possession and started to haul his equipment away. The beleaguered dentist got so upset watching the moving men drag his livelihood away that he blew out several blood vessels in his head and ended up in the hospital.

Bartowski, out of business and bankrupt, is currently making cappuccino at a Palm Springs coffeehouse. He has a malpractice claim pending against the negligent attorney.

The dentist learned the hard way that bankruptcy is a life-changing event and that before you plunge into it, you must have some knowledge of its consequences and plan for the future. It is, after all, major surgery, and second opinions ought to be obtained.

## Why Declare Bankruptcy?

This is the fundamental question you *must* answer before initiating such an important legal process, and to do that, you must first know what bankruptcy can accomplish for you.

Title 11 of the federal Bankruptcy Code was designed to enable people who have run into serious economic difficulty to get a fresh start by wiping out some burdensome debts and to keep creditors from employing harassing tactics to collect on those debts.

There is an abundance of myths about the wonders of bankruptcy, among them:

1. It will erase all of your debts.
2. It will keep creditors from taking any of your property.
3. It will stop your ex-spouse from getting alimony or child support, expunge tax debts, and eradicate that student loan you have outstanding.
4. It will not hurt your credit rating.

What bankruptcy *will* do is:

1. Give you *temporary* relief by stopping the collection of

debts, demand for payment of debts, and legal actions against you, such as foreclosure or eviction, for the period of time that your case is being handled by the court. This is called the "automatic stay." But you must be able to prove that you can make the payments on your car, furniture, and house if you expect to keep them.

2. Allow you to exempt *some* of your property, i.e., put it out of the reach of your creditors. Federal exemptions include such things as the value of your home up to $7,500 and one motor vehicle valued up to $1,200. Exemption rules in the state in which you reside, however, may be much more lenient than federal rules and may exempt more of your property.

3. Eliminate "dischargeable" debts. A dischargeable debt is one that you will no longer owe if you qualify for bankruptcy. Not all debts are dischargeable, only those determined by the court to be; those that are not can be subject to collection after you come out of bankruptcy.

4. Allow you to sue creditors who violate the "automatic stay" by bugging you for collection of a debt.

What it will *also* do is:

1. Appear in your credit history for ten years, making it difficult, if not impossible in some instances, to obtain credit or do anything that requires a sound credit rating. (This does not necessarily apply to obtaining credit cards, although your spending limit will certainly be restricted to a low amount.)

2. Make it almost impossible for you to obtain a mortgage by labeling you a foreclosure risk.

As the Bartowski case illustrates, before you file for bankruptcy, it is important to determine whether less drastic options are open to you. Bartowski did not need to file Chapter 11; in fact, he should *not* have filed. He would have been much better off consulting first with a debt counseling service, such as Consumer Credit Counseling Services.

CCCS is a national, nonprofit organization with state and local branches that provides debt counseling, budget planning, and debt consolidation for a nominal fee. Its staff will go over your financial status and discuss your options, including whether bankruptcy makes sense for you. If it does, they can provide you with the names of competent bankruptcy attorneys, or, in many cases, they will handle your bankruptcy filing for you, usually for a much lower fee than an attorney would charge.

To locate your closest CCCS office, call 1-800-388-CCCS.

In addition to CCCS, there are other private firms that provide similar services for a price. Look in the yellow pages under "Credit and Debt Counseling."

## Types of Bankruptcy

### Chapter 7

This is the type of bankruptcy that is filed for by the average consumer who has run up so many credit card charges or other debts, whether by mismanagement, misfortune, or otherwise, that there is no other way out. Creditors can garnish wages, making it impossible for you to hold a job or pay rent or a mortgage, and if you can't work out your financial problems through normal channels, Chapter 7 might be your only alternative.

While it will give you a fresh start in life, it is major surgery. In the computerized society in which we live, credit reporting agencies will furnish bankruptcy filing information to any and all companies to which you apply for credit for years into the future. In most cases, you will find it difficult, if not impossible, to purchase a home, and if you wish to buy a car for anything other than cash, interest charges will be astronomical.

But the picture under Chapter 7 may not be totally bleak. For example, if you own a home that is subject to a mortgage and can keep up the payments, provided other debts are discharged, the mortgage holder cannot take the house away from you. The same holds true for furniture and modestly priced automobiles on which you are making payments. However, if you fail to keep your payments current, you will lose those assets, too.

Under Chapter 7, all unsecured debts, such as doctor, dentist, legal, and credit card bills, are wiped out. You can become free of debt for all bills except child support, alimony, and income taxes.

Each state has different laws which allow debtors to keep various types of assets, and anyone considering this type of bankruptcy would be well advised to become familiar with his state's exemption statutes before deciding to make such a drastic move.

In Chapter 7 proceedings, a trustee is appointed to take charge of all nonexempt property (take note: an income tax refund check is a nonexempt asset) and will sell off all such property to the highest bidder. The debts will be discharged through the sale proceeds, but you will be left without credit.

## Chapter 13

If you have a steady job and have a house you're trying to hold on to, Chapter 13 bankruptcy allows you to reorganize your affairs and work out a plan to pay off your creditors over a period of years, usually five. You can file under Chapter 13 if you have unsecured debts under $100,000 and secured debts under $350,000. If, however, the court does not approve your payoff plan or you find yourself unable to pay the debts according to your plan, your Chapter 13 filing will most likely be converted to Chapter 7, and some of your assets will be subject to liquidation.

## Chapter 11

Chapter 11 is a more complicated process, reserved for businesses or people who have more assets than the Chapter

13 limits. Chapter 11 relief is usually in the form of reorganization or liquidation of both secured and unsecured debts. Chapter 11 is a very complicated process and should never be undertaken without the aid of an attorney experienced and competent in Chapter 11 filings.

## Doing It Yourself

With the recession-driven increase in bankruptcies has come a proliferation of books and manuals on how to file bankruptcy on your own. Since a person contemplating a step as drastic as bankruptcy is by definition strapped for cash, the thought of eliminating attorney's fees may be superficially appealing. There is an old cliché, however: Don't be penny-wise and pound-foolish. The dangers of filing on your own are much greater than the few hundreds dollars you would pay an expert to lead you through the process.

The bankruptcy process requires that you file a bankruptcy petition, notices, debt schedules, and property schedules on official forms, *completely, properly, and on time*. Each creditor whose debts you are trying to discharge must be given proper notice of your intent to file so that he or she will be able to appear against you in court and oppose your bankruptcy. You cannot give this notice yourself. It will be mailed by the clerk of the bankruptcy court.

To declare bankruptcy, you must have resided in the bankruptcy court district where you file the action for at least three months and one day.

These are only a few of the pitfalls you may encounter filing on your own. Any one of them can result in your case being thrown out of court or cause you major financial losses you might have avoided with the help of expert advice. A competent attorney can not only increase the odds that the surgery will be a success, he or she can also make sure the scar that you will live with for years is smaller. In addition, the attorney can help alleviate the emotional stress that necessarily comes with such an event. A person contemplating bankruptcy has enough to worry about without taking on the extra anxiety of dealing with the technicalities of law.

If you insist on going forward, there are, as we said, texts available to lead you through the process. Two such are *How to File Bankruptcy*, Nolo Press, 950 Parker Street, Berkeley, CA 94710-9867, (510) 549-1976; and *The Non-Lawyers Bankruptcy Kit*, Alpha Publications, P.O. Box 12488, Tucson, AZ 85732-2488, (800) 528-3494. (Alpha, which like Nolo, has a line of other legal self-help kits, advertises itself as the only publisher with a toll-free help line to answer consumer questions about its books.)

These and most other self-help bankruptcy manuals cover only Chapter 7 filings. Chapter 13 is a much more complicated process, and most people who attempt it on their own wish too late they hadn't. Before you plunge ahead, you might be wise to invest $80 in *Consumer Bankruptcy Law and Practice*, which covers *most* of what you need to know about Chapter 13 filings. You can order it by calling the National Consumer Law Center, (617) 523-8010. After reading the book and seeing the legal hoops you will have to jump through, you will probably come to the conclusion that you would have been better off putting your eighty bucks toward legal fees.

### Paralegals and Typing Services

In states in which they can legally offer services, paralegals can help you prepare your bankruptcy petition and forms. In some cases, they can also help you organize your debts and list of creditors. They cannot, however, offer you legal advice, nor can they appear in court for you. Once they type up your papers, you're on your own. The average charge for such a service is around $150.

Like a bad attorney, an incompetent paralegal can botch up your case by improperly preparing forms. Still, it must be said that in many cases, the *attorney* you hire may be using a paralegal in his office to prepare your forms. So if your Chapter 7 case is simple and straightforward, you might be just as well off going the paralegal route and saving the money. If you do use a paralegal service, make sure the outfit offers an unconditional money-back guarantee if you aren't satisfied. And be aware of the risks.

## How to Find Your Bankruptcy Attorney

Just as you wouldn't be wise to take out your own appendix, neither would you be wise to hire a veterinarian to do it. Just because a lawyer has a framed plaque on his wall licensing him to practice law, does not mean he is qualified to handle your bankruptcy case. Bankruptcy is a specialized field and, since what is at stake are your assets and since you are going to dish out attorney's fees to whomever you hire, it makes sense to find an attorney both experienced and competent in bankruptcy law. As a rule of thumb, look for an attorney who is a bankruptcy specialist and who has been practicing bankruptcy law for at least five years. There are a lot of attorneys out there who would be very willing to *learn* how to file a bankruptcy case; let them do it on someone else's dime.

In addition to the previously mentioned referral sources in chapter 5, a valuable source of information is your nearest CCCS office. If you don't want the CCCS staff to handle your bankruptcy case, or if it is too complicated for them, they should be able to refer you to a number of competent attorneys.

You might also try contacting a Chapter 7 or 13 trustee. Trustees are individuals appointed by the court to review your financial information, petition, and schedules, and in some cases to evaluate your payment plans. You can locate these people by telephoning the United States Trustee's office in your federal bankruptcy district and asking for a referral to a good attorney. Although a trustee ordinarily will be reluctant to refer you to a particular attorney, ask him or her for a list of half a dozen qualified lawyers. You might get lucky.

### Avoid Like the Plague

*Attorneys who have ever been disciplined by the bar or put on probation.* All this takes is a phone call to your local bar. Incompetent and crooked lawyers are usually repeat offenders, and although the bar is notoriously slow to mete out punishment to its members, infractions resulting in reprimands, fines, and temporary suspension to practice law are a matter of public record.

One recent example was L.A. lawyer Lon B. Isaacson, who was suspended from practicing law in 1994 and put on two years' probation for failing to provide accounting to clients, revealing clients' confidences, and overcharging for services. In one 1988 case, Isaacson had been hired to file bankruptcy by a client whose house was in foreclosure. He collected $5,270, but the client's case was dismissed for failure to make post-petition payments. As a result, the client lost her home. Another couple's bankruptcy was thrown out of court because of delinquent plan payments by Isaacson, leaving them facing a foreclosure on their home.

In all, Isaacson had sixteen such infractions dating back to 1982, but it took the California Bar twelve years to suspend him, and then for only sixty days! Any of those clients could perhaps have avoided personal disaster if they'd only taken the time to pick up a phone and inquire about their prospective lawyer.

*Attorneys who actively solicit your business.* Just as there are "ambulance chasers" in the personal injury business, there are "bankruptcy chasers" in the bankruptcy field, especially since the bankruptcy boom of the 1980s. These lawyers constantly comb through public records of recent home foreclosures, defaults, or notices of unlawful detainer filed by landlords against tenants who owe them rent. Since the addresses as well as the names of the people being sued are listed, form letters are sent out to every defendant offering the attorney's (or sometimes paralegal's) services to get the judgment stayed by filing bankruptcy.

A bankruptcy lawyer who contacts you is merely looking for business, so expect to be treated by him/her as you would by any other hustler. His interest is money—how to separate you from whatever you have left—so don't be surprised when you find the final tally is more than you were led to expect.

*Any lawyer who wants you to sign over a second trust deed on your home to secure his legal fees.* This practice was recently declared illegal by the Bankruptcy Code due to an abundance of attorney abuses. If the attorney brings this up, it is a sure sign he is a crook.

*Slick TV advertisers.* More often than not, the operations of these lawyers are nothing but bankruptcy mills staffed mostly by secretaries and paralegals who fill out the forms. The lawyer or lawyers working there are frequently incompetent or are employed only to prevent the operation from being prosecuted for the illegal practice of law.

One egregious example of such a firm was Davis and Associates of San Antonio, Texas, which carried on a slick local TV campaign promoting itself as a dynamic attorney group specializing in bankruptcy. In fact, there was only one lawyer employed by the firm, and he was inexperienced in the field. Intake interviews were conducted by paralegals, who were paid bonuses for the clients they signed up and who made the decision for the clients whether to file under Chapter 7 or 13. Clients whose cases were routinely handled (and bungled) by secretaries were charged $1,500 for a standard Chapter 7 filing. In 1993, after the owner (a nonlawyer) left town with the clients' money, Davis and Associates was barred by the court from practicing bankruptcy law in West Texas. Unfortunately, it was too late for those Davis and Associates clients who lost their lawyers' fees and, in many cases, their property.

## The First Interview

When you walk through the office doors of your prospective attorney, look around. Does the office have a factory atmosphere, the rooms filled with cubicles staffed by secretaries? After you announce your wish to see Attorney X, are you taken to see Paralegal Bob, who asks you questions and begins to fill out forms? Does Attorney X keep you waiting a long time? Is his appearance when you finally get to see him a little threadbare? Does he seem distracted, accept phone calls during your interview, seem to lack interest in your case, or try to turn you over to one of the staff? Take a walk.

During the initial interview, have as much information with you about your debts and your financial situation as you can get together. A good attorney should have a list of cogent questions about your predicament and should be able to tell you up front which of your debts is dischargeable. If he or she doesn't ask questions, is vague or evasive, or has to pull a book down off a shelf for reference, take a walk.

One matter you should get straight with your attorney immediately is how much you will be charged. By this, I don't mean the attorney's standard fee, but what he will charge *in toto*.

Most lawyers will charge a flat fee for Chapter 7 cases, ranging from $500 to over $1,000. (In addition to lawyer's fees, you will also be required to pay a $150 court filing fee for Chapter 7 or 13 cases.) Even if an attorney does not wish to discuss your case over the phone, she should not be reluctant to state her normal charge (even within a range) for *routine* Chapter 7 cases. If the attorney tries to avoid the question by telling you that it is impossible to give you any pricing parameters until you come into the office, hang up and let your fingers do some more walking.

Because of its complicated nature, Chapter 13 is a different story, and such reluctance is not necessarily unreasonable or surprising. Attorney's fees for Chapter 13 are usually more—sometimes quite a bit more—and the attorney will almost assuredly want to talk to you in person to get a clearer picture of your financial situation before discussing charges.

What the client must watch out for is hidden costs. In both Chapter 7 and 13 filings, as in any legal proceeding, what costs the attorney money is time. If one of your creditors goes to court to object to the discharge of your debt, the resulting lawsuit can take some time and effort by your attorney to fight. To hedge their bets, some attorneys will try to protect their profit margins by excluding some kinds of work from the basic fee. Always find out just what the attorney intends to do for his fee and what little extras are not included. And remember the cardinal rule: *Get it in writing.*

*Make sure you let your attorney know you expect no surprises down the line.* Some attorneys try to suck in clients with low up-front charges and sock it to them later with add-ons. Even an ethical attorney who gets into your case and finds he misjudged the complexity or time he will have to devote to you might try to charge you more than the agreed-to fee. *Don't fall for it.*

Remember, once committed to your cause, an attorney cannot arbitrarily drop you as a client. By law, the attorney must continue to represent you until you find another attorney or the court releases him or her from your case.

In addition, you have other remedies. If you think you've been ripped off by your attorney, you can ask the bankruptcy judge whether you have been overcharged. If the attorney botched the case or charged excessive fees for services rendered, the judge may order the lawyer to return all or part of what you paid him.

You can also make a request for a fee adjustment through

your Chapter 7 or 13 trustee, and ask him to present the request to your bankruptcy judge.

Attorneys hate being admonished by judges before whom they regularly appear, so you might try to discuss the overcharges with the attorney before you resort to official action. You might find him more amenable to compromise than you thought.

# 9 Criminal Law

One area of law you absolutely must have the most capable representation for is criminal law. If you are charged with a crime, you can lose the most precious commodity you own—your freedom. Thousands of people go to jail every year because their criminal attorneys were inept, lazy, or downright stupid.

The importance of having a competent criminal attorney in your corner *from the outset of your case* is even greater if you're innocent. As a criminal attorney who has tried every kind of case, including over fifty homicide cases (twenty were acquitted), one of the authors (D.G.) has witnessed many times the tragic results of an innocent person being asked by the police, "Do you want an attorney?" and answering, "Why would I need an attorney? I didn't do anything." Without the aid of a good criminal attorney, an innocent person can easily get railroaded straight into prison.

*Remember: Nobody cares if you're innocent—not the cops, not the prosecutor, not even your own attorney.* In fact, if you are innocent, the burden on your attorney will be greater in that he or she will not have the option of plea bargaining your case, and the workload to get an acquittal will be greater. With criminal attorneys, the game is money. With cops and prosecutors, the game is to rack up enough arrests and convictions to make them look good in the eyes of the higher-ups. To both sides, the criminal justice system is nothing but a game, and you are a pawn on the board.

There is an old expression in criminal legal circles that pertains especially to the defense of serious crimes: "The practice of criminal law is similar to a doctor who specializes in cancer—the outlook is dim, but you can at least buy some time."

## Types of Crimes

The dictionary definition of a crime is "an action or an instance of negligence that is deemed injurious to the public welfare or morals, or to the interests of the state, and that is legally prohibited."

What constitutes a crime varies from state to state, although some acts, like murder, are illegal in all fifty states. There are two major categories of crime:

1. *Misdemeanors* are less serious crimes, such as driving under the influence, shoplifting, petty theft, writing bad checks, drunkenness in public, or trespassing. Misdemeanors make up the bulk of the criminal court docket and are the types of crimes of which the average citizen or first-time offender might find himself accused.

2. *Felonies* are more serious crimes, like burglary, murder, manslaughter, robbery, narcotics dealing, and major frauds. These types of crimes are usually perpetrated by experienced

criminals who are constantly being processed by the system. (Strangely, the majority of people accused of killing another human being have never been in jail in their lives. Murder most frequently erupts from violent emotions between loved ones, friends, neighbors, relatives, and business associates.)

Both types of crime have various degrees of seriousness. The punishment for conviction of a misdemeanor is usually a monetary fine and sometimes, depending upon the degree of the crime and the record of the defendant, a maxiumum of a year in the county jail. Felonies carry much harsher fines and almost always jail time—in state or federal prison.

If you're a professional criminal, you probably already have been represented in court by a lawyer or several lawyers, and you know whom to call when you get popped for bank robbery. Joe Q. Citizen, however, who has had no contact with the criminal justice system, usually has no idea where to turn when he gets pulled in for driving after one too many.

*Don't waste your phone call from jail calling an attorney unless you already know who you want to represent you.* An attorney will only call a bail bondsman to get you out. You can do that yourself. After you are out and away from the dehumanizing experience of being in jail, you can pick your attorney.

## Who Not to Call

### Corporate or Other Noncriminal Attorneys

Most criminal attorneys practice nothing but criminal law. That is because most of them are former district attorneys or public defenders, and they know nothing else. Occasionally a lawyer from a large firm specializing in corporate law will attempt to handle a white-collar crime case for one of the firm's clients—and will invariably botch it.

Some high-profile attorneys, like Melvin Belli, will handle civil as well as criminal cases. We strongly advise against hiring any lawyer to handle a criminal case who splits his time between specialties. If you are accused of a felony, or even a misdemeanor, and face the possibility of a ruined reputation and perhaps real jail time, you wouldn't want your attorney to be distracted by the big bucks he's going to get settling that personal injury lawsuit he's got on his desk.

Let's take a typical example of how putting your trust in a noncriminal lawyer can lead to disaster. A few years ago, Sylvia Fielding,* the wife of a prominent L.A. plastic surgeon, was pulled over after a party for driving recklessly. After refusing to take a field sobriety test, she was taken to jail and administered a breath sample test.

Mrs. Fielding was given a ticket for drunk driving, which she took to a corporate lawyer friend of the family who was a senior partner at a large, prestigious Beverly Hills firm. The lawyer did some checking and found out that her breath test showed her blood alcohol level to have been .22—a very high reading—even though she swore she'd had only two glasses of champagne an hour earlier. The attorney, knowing he couldn't beat such a high reading, extracted $3,500 from the woman and sent one of his junior associates to court to plead her guilty.

Two weeks later, a veteran criminal lawyer got a DUI client who had been taken to the same jail as Mrs. Fielding and had also gotten a .22 on the breath test. The criminal lawyer's client had two priors and was facing major penalties if convicted. The criminal lawyer, while not particularly a genius, did what any experienced defense attorney would routinely do—got the number of the breath sample machine off the police report and sent a formal demand for the device's maintenance records.

These records indicated that during the time Mrs. Fielding and the criminal attorney's client took their breath tests, forty other people in a row had readings of .22. The machine, it seems, had been sent back to the manufacturer for repair.

The defense attorney's client ended up pleading guilty to an unsafe lane change.

Mrs. Fielding, in the meantime, because of her lawyer's inexperience and incompetence, ended up with a $1,000 fine, probation, and an "at risk driver" rating, resulting in years of costly accident insurance premiums.

## The Big Guns

These are the high-profile, publicity-seeking Perry Masons who somehow always seem to be in the media spotlight representing celebrities' scandals. They frequently write books (or more likely, dictate them) about their magnificent courtroom triumphs (often, the cases are surprisingly old) and appear regularly on talk shows. They are never shy to express an opinion on "Nightline" about a colleague's handling of the hot case of the day.

Few knowledgeable attorneys, if accused of a crime, would hire any of these hotshots to defend them. More likely than not, the Big Guns are from out of town and don't know the local judges or prosecutors. That can be a *huge* disadvantage coming in. Rather than being impressed, the judge may be turned off by the Big Gun's reputation, which invariably precedes him, and his demeanor in court, which is often egotistical and condescending.

Another factor to take into account when you consider hiring this kind of attorney is the fee, which will undoubtedly be twice what a less known, competent criminal attorney will charge for better results.

By the way, these Big Guns *will* handle your case if you want, no matter how small. While these lawyers may handle an occasional celebrity's case, 50 percent of their caseload will be drunk drivers. Just don't expect the Big Gun to represent you in court; he will assign an underling to your case, but charge you as if he were there himself.

## Court-Appointed Attorneys

According to the law, if you cannot afford to pay an attorney to represent you, the state will appoint one for you at its expense. You can usually spot these guys hanging around the halls of the courtroom like vultures, waiting for an appointment.

Usually, judges will appoint the same few lawyers over and over to represent various clients. These lawyers are known in the trade as roundheels, because they roll over easily on every charge. Judges like them because they know they are going to make their lives easier. They will never take a case to trial, they won't make a lot of motions which the judge will have to rule on, and they'll grind the client down quickly to cop a plea so the judge can keep his afternoon golf date.

## Courthouse Hustlers

These guys hang around the court at arraignment time, sizing up the defendants. Through years of experience, they have an instinctive ability to pick out the defendants who are not represented by counsel, and will immediately pounce on them, card in hand. Their approach will often be deceivingly benign: "I see you have a DUI. If you have any questions, I'd be glad to answer them, free of charge." Once you're reeled in, nothing will be free of charge.

Or they may try scare tactics to get you hooked. "Don't dare cop a guilty plea in front of this judge," this lawyer whispers in your ear. "He'll put you away."

Now that you're good and worried, you ask, "What do I do?"

"Plead not guilty and we'll get you in front of another judge."

The defendant, who is usually humiliated and emotionally drained from spending a night in jail and bewildered by the entire judicial process, has no idea that once he pleads "not guilty," the case would be signed out to another judge anyway. He also is not aware that an arraignment judge is usually the most lenient in his sentencing for the simple reason that if he's "Lock 'em Up Joe," word will get around and *everybody* will be pleading "not guilty," jamming up the court calendar.

You can usually spot the Courthouse Hustler by his worn briefcase, his scuffed shoes, and the predatory glint in his eye.

### Attorneys Who Are Afraid to Go to Trial

This may sound funny, but it is a sad fact that a lot of attorneys are afraid to go to trial. They tried a few cases, got trounced, and are terrified of repeating the experience.

Less than 10 percent of the lawyers in this country have tried five cases in their entire careers. We've known lawyers who have gotten the cold sweats just *thinking* about going to trial and who will not try a case under any circumstances. In civil cases, these lawyers always settle. In criminal cases, they try to talk their clients into plea bargains—deals with the DA for lighter sentences in exchange for guilty pleas. These professional plea bargainers will seldom get the best deal for their clients, simply because the prosecutors know these plea bargainers will never slug it out in court. The way to tell if you have one of these clowns as a lawyer is if he tries to get you to cop a plea too quickly.

This is not to say that an attorney who recommends a plea bargain is a bad attorney or afraid of battle. One of the best attributes of a criminal defense attorney is his ability to plea bargain to the best advantage for his client, especially if the prosecution's case is overwhelming.

### The Miracle Worker

This is the guy who in the face of inevitable, looming disaster promises he can lead you to safety.

About fifteen years ago, one of the authors (D.G.) had a

case in which a young lad was caught trafficking a sizable load of marijuana. There was no way around the evidence, but since the kid was a first-time offender, I told him that the best course he could take was to plead guilty, after which he would be sentenced to state prison. I informed him that since state prisons were so crowded, the penal system was lenient on nonviolent criminals. I told him to enter a plea of guilty. As part of a plea bargain, he would get a psychiatric evaluation that would in all likelihood show that he was not dangerous or a menace to society and would be a suitable candidate for parole. The entire process, I told him, would take about five months.

Shortly thereafter, I was contacted by the boy's father, who happened to be a friend of mine, and was told that he was hiring another attorney. My friend apologized, but said that his son was too sensitive to go to state prison and that he had been guaranteed by another attorney that for a price he could get the boy straight probation. Knowing there was no way the kid was going to get probation for selling dope in that kind of quantity, I asked who the new attorney would be. When I heard the name of the man, I laughed and asked how much it was going to cost.

"Five thousand," my friend said.

"How much have you already paid him?"

"Fifteen hundred."

I shook my head. "All he's going to do is take your money and get you the same results."

My friend was adamant. "I was with the attorney when he went back into the judge's chambers. He made a deal. It's set."

The scam was the same one this attorney had been running for years on desperate clients with hopeless situations. Usually, he would work the sting in his office, where he would inform the hapless client, "They got you dead-bang. You're going to the joint. There's one possibility: Maybe we can buy you probation. It's gonna cost ten grand. You might think that's steep, but not all this money winds up in my pocket. It gets spread around, you get me?"

At this point, he would press a button under the desk that would cause the phone to ring. He would pick up the phone, which was dead, and say, "Just a minute, Judge."

He'd cup the phone and tell the gullible client to be real quiet, then get back to the fake phone conversation. "Yeah, Judge, I got the money. Meet me at the same place. Now, I want to make sure we're talking probation. Ninety days? Sure, I understand, you can't take too much heat. Don't worry, this guy can do ninety days standing on his head."

When he hung up, he'd tell the client, "I'll need $25,000 within thirty days, all in hundreds."

If the client was a burglar, he'd go out and take down some houses to make the money. And in the end, he'd plead guilty and go to the slammer for the maximum time.

This particular lawyer had worked this same deal on so many clients that they all got together in prison and called the IRS on the attorney for income tax evasion. He eventually beat the tax rap on a search warrant technicality and is still running the same scam—along with his attorney son, who is a chip off the old block.

My client with the marijuana beef? He pleaded guilty and as part of the plea bargain was sentenced to state prison for a five-month diagnostic study, after which he was released on probation.

## How to Find the Right Criminal Attorney

### Always Hire Local

We can't stress this enough. Criminal attorneys who practice regularly in local courts know how the game is played. They have connections and relationships with the police department and the DA's office that an out-of-towner will not have. He or she will usually be able to expedite getting reports and know which judges are "hanging judges" and which are more lenient.

As an example, I tried many cases in the court of one L.A. County Superior Court judge who tended to go lenient on your client if you pleaded him guilty. If you went to jury trial and lost, however, he would mete out the maximum sentence every time. His reputation was well known to anyone who had tried a case in his court, but because his manner was so low-key, to some out-of-town attorney he would seem like just a nice old guy—until the sentencing.

## Referrals

These can be gotten from the usual places, plus a few we haven't mentioned.

Anybody who conducts business around criminal courts knows who is reputable and good—judges, court clerks, bailiffs, stenographers. If you have a friend who is a DA or a cop, ask him or her for a recommendation. DA's know their opposition, and cops, having testified as prosecution witnesses, will also know who is effective at cross-examination. Again, tell the person you are asking for a referral the general nature of the charges against you. A lawyer who is a whiz with DUIs might not be as good for a narcotics possession charge. And few criminal attorneys have the skills and business understanding to handle the complexities of an intricate white-collar-crime case such as major securities fraud.

Public defenders are paid by the state to represent indigent defendants. In most cities and counties, they are prohibited from handling private clients, but they are constantly in the courtroom and know who is good and who is not. Contact a public defender in person or by telephone, tell him the kind of case you have, and ask for a referral. Often, he will give you one or more names, and such recommendations are usually reliable.

## Courtroom Observations

During your arraignment, or well in advance of your court date, you might spend a morning at the courthouse observing the conduct of the various defense lawyers. Not only will you see them in action, but you will get accustomed to the courtroom atmosphere and perhaps defuse some of the anxiety you will inevitably experience during the "real" trial. Watch the judges' body language and rulings when various attorneys make motions. Experienced judges know clod lawyers; they know who comes prepared and who doesn't. The ones who don't make the judges' jobs more difficult, and the judges' reactions often betray that fact. If the rulings are more negative than not, or if the judge reacts to a certain lawyer in a consistently cold or unfriendly manner, you might want to avoid that attorney.

# The Initial Interview

Ask your attorney how he became a criminal lawyer. He will probably tell you he used to be with the DA's office and left because the pay stunk. That's fine; in fact, if he was with the local DA's office and he didn't leave too long ago, he probably still has connections and friendships there he can cash in on for you. An ex-DA has also probably had a lot of trial experience, at least if he or she spent any length of time in the public sector.

Find out if your attorney is willing to scrap. Ask how many jury trials the attorney has had during the past twenty-four months and how many court trials. Ask for the outcomes and for some of the names of the defendants. If the lawyer tells you that that information is confidential, point out that the disposition of all criminal cases is public information. If he still gives you the stall, reconsider hiring him.

If you get past that hurdle and you still like what you're hearing, lay out your case. Even if you don't hire him, whatever you tell him is confidential.

*That doesn't necessarily mean you have to admit to him you're guilty.* A good defense attorney will never ask you that question—he doesn't really want to know. What he *should* want to know is the facts surrounding your case, your frame of mind at the time the crime took place, and what you told the cops.

Ask him what maximum penalties you will face if you are found guilty, including fines and loss of privileges, such as a driver's license.

If the crime you're accused of is not unique, such as drunk driving, petty theft, or even manslaughter, and he has to consult a book, he should *not* be defending you. If you are charged with bestiality, however, he may never have run across such a case before, and reaching for the penal code might not necessarily put him out of the running.

Ask him what your chances are of beating the rap. If he says he thinks he has a pretty good chance of winning your case, says it with enthusiasm and conviction, and has a good track record with your kind of case, you might want to hire him.

If he says your case is hopeless, ask him what he can do for you that you can't accomplish for yourself by going to court and pleading guilty. If he tells you he can probably get your charges reduced or prior convictions stricken from your record, you still might want to consider hiring him.

On the other hand (and it does occasionally happen), the lawyer may tell you there is nothing he can do that you can't do alone. In that case, pay him for his time, take a lot of his business cards to hand out to your friends, and mail one of them to Diogenes. You've just found an honest man.

If you hire the attorney, immediately get the fees straight. Criminal attorneys, because of the uncertain future of their clients, will always want to be paid up front. If you are an upstanding citizen who has never been in trouble before, or a first-timer and the charges aren't that serious, you might be able to work out some sort of payment schedule. That courtesy will almost never be extended to professional criminals. After all, they got their money by beating somebody else out of it, and few would have any compunction about beating their lawyer out of it.

Fees among criminal attorneys vary widely, according to reputation and what the traffic will bear. Flat fee arrangements are most common, based on the level to which the case is taken: X for a simple plea bargain, one court appearance; Y for pretrial; Z for a full-blown jury trial. Call around to get some general information about the going rates for your type of case.

Get it all down in a contract, just as you would with an attorney representing you in a civil matter. (A sample criminal attorney contract is in Appendix B.)

*Warning:* Good and reputable criminal attorneys will not vary their rates and will be upfront with you, even if their fees are expensive; sleazeball attorneys will smell the fear you exude and will charge accordingly. If you are panicky, they will mark up the price to whatever they think you will pay. Some of these crooks will use the Fear Factor once the fireworks have started in order to squeeze every drop of blood out of you they can.

A few years ago, an acquaintance of ours was falsely indicted for murder. In the middle of the pretrial phase, her attorney pulled her to one side and told her he wanted more money, otherwise he was going to have to quit the case. The poor woman, who had already paid him more than $100,000, panicked and signed over a couple of rental properties to the crook. The case was tossed out in pretrial, but the woman ended up paying almost half a million for nothing.

She didn't know it, but the lawyer could not have quit the case. Although a lawyer can leave a case, he cannot quit at a crucial time. Even if the case is not at a crucial stage, in some instances the lawyer must seek permission from the court to quit. Once a lawyer is in the process of defending you, he has to see the case through and defend you to the best of his ability. Any lawyer who tries to get more money out of you than you agreed upon and uses the threat of quitting or blowing your case is nothing more than an extortionist, and you should turn him in to the bar.

## Nolo Contendere

Most people don't know that they don't have to plead guilty or not guilty, but can enter a *nolo* plea. Basically, the defendant is saying that he will not contest the charges against him, but he is not admitting guilt. For the purposes of the criminal justice system, a *nolo* plea is tantamount to "guilty," and the sentencing will be the same as if the defendant pleaded guilty. If your chances of winning your case are slim and there looms the possibility of a civil suit as a result of your conviction, you might want to consider pleading *nolo*. That way, you have not admitted guilt and anyone who wants to sue you later is going to have to go to the trouble of proving you were guilty of the crime of which you were accused.

Let's take an example. Say you had too many beers one night and while driving home got into an accident in which someone else was injured. That other person is likely to come at you later and sue you for compensatory and punitive damages. If you plead guilty, you've admitted you were drunk, and the plaintiff's attorney has you by the short hairs. If you plead *nolo* you will get the same sentence from the court, but it doesn't affect your civil suit. The plaintiff has to prove you were drunk, that you were driving, and that your actions caused his or her injury. It makes the process more difficult, lengthy, and costly for the other side and will possibly increase the likelihood of a settlement.

## Warning Signs

Aside from the alarm bells previously mentioned, you should get yourself another attorney *immediately* if:

- He immediately says, "Let's plead guilty."

  (There are extraordinary cases that are exceptions to the general rule. For example, if the DA makes a mistake and files misdemeanor drunk driving charges against you when a personal injury was involved that would normally have resulted in the case being filed as a felony, your attorney should tell you to cop a guilty plea immediately, before the complaint can be amended. By your pleading guilty, jeopardy has been attached, and amending the complaint constitutes double jeopardy. Similarly, if a complaint against you alleges manslaughter when the true facts would disclose murder, plead guilty. In these instances, your attorney should explain in detail the reasons for an early plea.)

- Within two weeks of hiring him, you ask him for a copy of the police report and he doesn't have it. If the attorney hasn't bothered to make that easy and fundamental move, your case is very low on his list of priorities.

- After a month, you learn from your attorney that he has not bothered to contact or take statements from witnesses in your case. If he says he has, ask to see the statements. If he says he has, but cannot show you the statements (he might say they are being transcribed), or if you have reason to believe he is lying to you, have a friend call one or more of the witnesses (their names should be in the police report) and make sure the friend only asks the question whether or not the lawyer or his investigator has been in contact. You do not want to do this yourself, as you might be accused of intimidating a witness. If the attorney has not been in touch he/she might not be doing his/her job.

- After a reasonable amount of time, you ask the attorney if he has made a demand for discovery to find out what evidence the prosecution has against you and he says he has been too busy. Most experienced criminal attorneys have standard forms to get police reports, breath test records, and similar items. If the lawyer says he has made the demand, ask to see the photocopies. If he cannot produce them, get another lawyer.
- He shows up late in court without notifying you or the judge. On the other hand, some lawyers know that when a judge says eight-thirty, he really means nine-thirty, so if they both show up an hour late, you might still be okay.

# 10 Personal Injury

In 1989, a construction worker named Jerry May was at his home in San Diego, recuperating from a terrible fall he had sustained on a job site. As he lay on his couch, contemplating his uncertain future with fear, and not knowing what to do about his debilitating injuries and mounting medical bills, an ad came on the TV:

> It's easy for an accident victim to feel lost. Who do you turn to if you've been injured in an accident or hurt on the job?
>
> You can rely on the law offices of Sam Spital. Our staff of professionals know the law. We help you obtain compensation for all losses including the degree and frequency of your pain and suffering.
>
> Don't try to settle your case alone. Let us work for you. Call me, Sam Spital, at 231-4848.

It sounded good to May, who made an appointment and

went to the offices of Sam Spital. After being interviewed by a young associate, May was assured that Spital would be personally handling his case. Little did May know that not only was Spital not personally handling his case, *nobody* was handling his case. No investigation of the accident site was ever made, no witnesses were ever deposed, no discovery was ever exercised. In fact, the case, like *all* of Spital's cases, was never intended to go to trial.

Court records would later show that what Spital ran was a settlement mill handling a thousand cases at any one time, with two hundred per lawyer and three hundred per paralegal. There was a strict office policy requiring associates to settle a minimum of ten cases a month for at least $250,000 a year. Associates were told to contact insurance adjusters as fast as possible and to settle as fast as possible *for any amount*. Spital even ran in-house contests for settling cases, awarding boat rides and vacations to the winners.

Although May's case was later estimated to be worth $2 million, on July 8, 1991, two weeks before his scheduled trial date, May was summoned to Spital's office and told he should accept a $70,000 settlement from the construction company, which after medical expenses and legal fees (Spital was to take one-third of the settlement, plus $1,700 for expenses) would have left him with a grand total of $2,000. May was further told that if he didn't agree to the settlement, Spital would quit the case, which he was entitled to do under his contract.

Betrayed and defeated, May finally caved in and was given as a reward a coffee cup with Spital's office logo on it and the slogan, "I'm tough, smart, and know the law."

Tears streaming down his face, May took his coffee cup and drove to his mother's house. After discussing his situation, it became clear to May that he'd been coerced into an agreement. He telephoned Spital to tell him he'd changed his mind. Spital told him to get another lawyer.

May's new lawyer, Jeff Estes, managed to get a much more favorable settlement for Jerry, and upon hearing about it, Spital advised Estes that he had a lien of $23,333 plus $1,700 in expenses on the settlement, for "services rendered." Estes accused Spital of fraud, misrepresentation, and malfeasance. Spital offered to take $2,000.

Instead of paying the two grand, Jerry May, good and mad now, hired the offices of Frega and Tiffany to go after Spital for malpractice. On the witness stand, Spital shockingly admitted that in spite of his TV claims of being an "experi- enced trial lawyer" and "knowing the law," *he had never tried a case in his life!* He also could not remember if he'd ever prepared a request for production of documents and admitted he'd never even appeared in court on a summary judgment motion.

Spital was ordered by the court to cough up $3 million to May—$2 million for compensatory damages and $1 million in punitive damages. Sam Spital declared bankruptcy and Jerry May is still awaiting payment.

Sam Spital is not the rule among personal injury lawyers, but unfortunately, he's not the exception, either. There are plenty of personal injury lawyers who advertise their legal skills—and plenty more who don't advertise—who are incapable of trying a case, and who have no intention of trying a case, and who from a monetary standpoint succeed in making up for their incompetence by settling cases in bulk. They simply take 30 to 50 percent of their clients' money by selling them down the river.

### Contingency versus Hourly Billing

Most attorneys work on a contingency basis on personal injury cases. There are certain advantages in this kind of arrangement for the client who has little money to pay an attorney up front and who can't afford to wage a long legal battle with a deep-pockets corporation or insurance company. The disadvantage is that he or she will lose a large chunk of any settlement in the end. *Less than 50 cents of every liability dollar—often considerably less—ends up in the pocket of the injured.*

Attorneys justify taking such a large percentage by claiming that they are gambling their time and money and if you get nothing, they get nothing. Well... not exactly. Even if your attorney took your case all the way to court and lost, you would probably get a bill for his or her expenses.

The fact is, however, that the attorney's gamble is minimal. In the United States, while 10,000 injury cases might be filed, 9,800 are settled, 100 are voluntarily dismissed, and only 100, or 1 percent, actually go to trial.

This isn't solely because of lawyers who don't like to try cases. Insurance companies today are anxious to settle cases because of recent outrageous jury awards for punitive damages. One recent example is the case of Stella Liebeck, who spilled a cup of McDonald's coffee on herself and was awarded $2.7 million in punitive damages because the coffee was "too hot." Now, thanks to Mrs. Liebeck, millions of people across the country will have to drink cold coffee. So the incentive from both sides is to settle. (On a motion for a new trial, the judge reduced Ms. Liebeck's award to $600,000, still a pretty nice reward!)

If you have been terribly injured and feel that the company, person, or insurance company is playing hardball with you, your only recourse may be to take the opposition to the mat. Your bills are likely in that event to run into a considerable sum, and paying your lawyer on a contingency basis makes sense. But if your injuries are not life-changing and you *want* to settle, why cut an attorney in on the take?

A few years ago, a friend of one of the authors (D.G.) was involved in a car accident in which the other driver ran a red light. My friend sustained some injuries and his new exotic sports car was totaled. Not asking for any "pain and suffering" compensation, my friend told the other driver's insurance company that he would sign a waiver in that respect—all he wanted was the cost of his car, $8,000, which he documented with detailed invoices. Because the car was unique and didn't appear in the standard Blue Book, which values cars, the insurance company refused his valuation and offered one half of the car's worth.

Angered by the insurance company's intransigence, he asked me to file suit. After reviewing the facts of the case, I became convinced that my friend had an almost certain case for damages, not only for the loss of his car, but for medical expenses as well as pain and suffering. I was also certain that the insurance company, once threatened with a lawsuit, would settle rather quickly. Because of a trial conflict, I was unable to take the case, but I referred him to another attorney whom I knew to be honest and a tenacious litigator. I told my friend *not* to hire the lawyer on a contingency basis, but to pay him his normal hourly rate, which he did. The insurance company ended up settling the case for $25,000. Attorney's fees and expenses totaled $3,500, or 14 percent of the settlement. If my friend had wanted to push for an extra $5,000, that percentage would have been even lower. The point here is, if you have the money to pay a lawyer up front and you intend to settle, it might be more cost-effective for you to pay his going rate.

There is another big drawback to hiring a lawyer on contingency. If the lawyer turns out to be a shyster or a moron or you just don't like the way he does business, you can fire him and get new representation, but Lawyer #1 can still come after you for *quantum meruit*—a reasonable value for services rendered. The problem here is that the attorney often differs with the client as to what is reasonable. Sam Spital tried that with Jerry May and lost, but others have won, leaving virtually nothing for the poor client.

## Settling Without an Attorney

Insurance companies are required as a matter of law to negotiate with an injured person in "good faith." If lawyers have contributed anything toward the betterment of Americans, it has been the massive judgments they have obtained against those companies which have acted in "bad faith" in dealing with clients. Insurance companies are now so frightened out of their wits that each year they pay millions of dollars out of reserves in an attempt to avoid charges of bad faith.

Turn this to your advantage by negotiating directly with your insurance adjuster. When he makes an offer, throw the fear of God into him by asking if it has been made in good faith and if it is the maximum the company has authorized him to pay for your lost wages, medical expenses—past, present, *and* future—and pain and suffering.

If he tells you his offer is indeed made in good faith, and the offer sounds good to you, tell him you will accept it provided he puts his statements to that effect *in writing*. Then present him with the form in Appendix E of this book, allowing a claimant to contest a settlement made in bad faith.

If the adjuster refuses, or if you feel he is trying to lowball you on the amount, you still have a place to go without hiring an attorney. Tell the adjuster you want to put the claim to arbitration without lawyers involved on either side. More than likely, his company will jump at it.

When an arbitrator experienced in personal injury law is chosen, the claimant appears before him or her with pertinent medical information, including a description of injuries, a prognosis, bills for treatment and expenses, and proof of loss of income. The insurance adjuster—not an attorney—will present the company's view of the case, and the arbitrator will decide the proper settlement amount.

Arbitration is actually not a dramatic departure from

what regularly takes place in courtrooms. Ninety percent of all injury cases are settled in judges' chambers on the eve of trial. The result of arbitration is that the injured person will probably receive more money in a shorter period of time and save himself the emotional stress of a courtroom battle.

## Hiring an Attorney

Personal injury is semi-specialized work, but you don't necessarily need a lawyer who does nothing but PI. In fact, if a lawyer does personal injury work exclusively, he might be running a Sam Spital–type settlement mill and your interests could be put at risk.

Look for someone who is smart, tenacious, and experienced in a courtroom. Stay away from:

- The 50 percent contingency boys. Thirty to 35 percent is more like it.
- An attorney whose card is given to you by the tow truck driver who towed your car. These guys are frequently on the payroll of PI attorneys and get fees for referrals.
- An attorney whose card is given to you while you are in the hospital by one of the nurses or attendants. Same reason.
- An attorney who himself hands you a card while you are in the hospital or who calls you up soliciting your business. He's an ambulance chaser.
- Must we say it? The guy on the slick TV ad. If an attorney is forking out big bucks on advertising, he is trying for high volume and is in all likelihood running a settlement mill. But there's another reason not to hire these jokers—the more they advertise, the less money they may get for you.

Studies in Florida and Nevada have indicated that jurors tend to look at advertising attorneys as greedy and seedy wheeler-dealers in justice. The result: less damages for their clients. A master's thesis study by Stephanie M. Myers analyzed fifty-four personal injury and medical malpractice trials in Las Vegas and found that jurors voted against plaintiffs whose lawyers advertised on TV more than twice as often as against plaintiffs who had nonadvertising lawyers. The study, although disputed by proponents of advertising, was enough to get Ms. Myers' husband, attorney Richard Myers, to dump his TV ads. Some attorneys now make it a point to inform a jury that opposing counsel is a TV advertiser, hoping it will have an adverse impact on the plaintiff's case, and conversely, huckster lawyers will often go to lengths to prohibit any mention in the courtroom that they're TV advertisers.

Once you've picked your attorney and it's down to nuts and bolts:

- In your retainer agreement, make sure it is spelled out that apart from your actual medical expenses for care and treatment of your injuries, *no expenses will be incurred or paid without your prior consent.*
- If you change attorneys midstream, make certain that the second lawyer will pay the fired attorney from *his* share of the settlement.
- Never sign a contract that allows the lawyer to drop your case if you refuse to accept his settlement advice.
- Never sign a contract that says you are liable for the attorney's expenses whether he wins or loses your case. Make the attorney *really* gamble—with his money, not yours.

## Trust Account Abuses

Personal injury cases are a little different from other cases in that when an attorney agrees to represent a client with an insurance or other claim, he or she sets up a trust account in the client's name into which is deposited any settlement money and any money the attorney may advance the client. From that account, the attorney writes checks to cover the client's expenses—medical, investigative, and so forth. When the insurance company and client agree on a settlement amount, a bank draft is usually made out jointly in the attorney's and client's names, and both of them have to endorse it before it goes into the account. This way, everybody is informed as to what is going on. After all the bills are paid off, the attorney and the client split what is left according to the agreed-upon percentage.

The most frequent abuses by unethical PI attorneys occur *before* the final reckoning. Crooked lawyers frequently have arrangements with crooked doctors whereby they pay grossly inflated medical bills with clients' money and take kickbacks from the doctors. They have also been known to pay money to dummy corporations, to phony private investigators who again kick back, and even to themselves.

If you allow an attorney to sign your name, you will have no idea how much the insurance company really paid him. If you've given the attorney the power to sign a release form, the insurance company can refuse to pay you, *even if you can prove that you didn't know what the attorney was doing or that the attorney stole your money*. If the attorney forges your name, however, the insurance company is still on the hook and has to pay you, even if the lawyer has raided the trust account.

A few years ago, one of the biggest ambulance-chasing operations in L.A. history was uncovered. Lawyers and doctors, working in a network, were found to be regularly screwing clients brought to them by an investigative firm which was really nothing more than a capping operation. ("Capping" is the illegal solicitation of personal injury claims.) The group would hire people to select innocent victims on the freeway, involve them in accidents, and then solicit the victims' business for certain attorneys. The attorneys would settle all the claims—the victims' and the investigator's employees'—and then rake off most of the proceeds through padded expenses and lawyer's fees. Settlements of $25,000 regularly turned into $1,000 for the accident victims, and often, after being paid off, the victims found that their medical bills had *not* been paid when they started getting hospital bills. This particular ring specialized in victimizing immigrants who did not read English particularly well and who had little understanding of the law or their rights.

Clients have very little protection from these kinds of abuses. About the most you can do when your case is settled is demand a full settlement document breaking down what was paid out, to whom, and for what. If you don't like what your lawyer gives you or if he is unresponsive, tell him you're going to report him or her to the bar. If you think you've been victimized illegally, threaten to turn him in to the D.A. A crooked lawyer doesn't like heat and might just find he made an "error" when adding up his expense sheet.

If he does give you a refund, turn him in to the bar and the D.A. anyway. If unchecked, that attorney will just be free to rip off more unsuspecting clients.

# 11 Divorce

Barry and Marjorie Macklin,* like many couples, had their problems after twelve years of marriage. They seemed to have grown apart, their silences grew longer, the sex was almost nonexistent. The intimacy and mutual admiration that they had felt in the beginning of their marriage had waned, leaving both of them to wonder if there was not something better out there waiting for them. Still, it was a shock to Barry when Marjorie told him over breakfast one day that she wanted a divorce.

Barry tried to talk her out of it. He thought divorce a drastic step that they would both regret, particularly when he thought about being apart from his three children. He suggested that they separate and seek counseling, but Marjorie was adamant. She informed him she had already hired an attorney and then put in front of Barry what the attorney had informed her was a fair settlement of their $150,000 estate.

She would get the house, the furnishings, one automobile, half of the money in the bank accounts, and custody of the children. Barry would get the boat and his car, and would pay $1,500 a month in child support as well as $900 a month in alimony for six years. Visitation rights for the children would be every other weekend.

In spite of the fact he didn't want to battle his wife in court, Barry, feeling there was a gun pointed at his head, hired his own attorney. The attorney looked at what was being offered and shook his head. "She wants too much," he told Barry. "The child support arrangement is out of line for starters. You can do much better."

If Barry was shocked when his wife told him she wanted to bail out, he was even more surprised when he got his attorney's first bill—$15,000 for "research." In the meantime, the attorney had not even filed a response to the divorce petition. What he had done was make a counteroffer to Marjorie Macklin's attorney which was so low that when she heard it, she became incensed. She told her attorney to go to war.

When the smoke of battle cleared, Barry Macklin's attorney's fees totaled $55,000. What that $55,000 bought him was child support payments within $95 of what his wife's lawyer had been asking, worse visitation rights, and a $5,000 difference in the property settlement—*in his wife's favor.*

## Lawyers and Divorce

Up until the late 1960s, divorce was granted in many states only by proving fault, such as desertion, physical or mental cruelty, or adultery. Since then, however, courts in most states have more humanely and rationally recognized that sometimes couples just can't cut it together, for no fault other than that they are who they are.

No-fault divorce, or *dissolution*, became accepted, and

divorce became easier and less accusatory. Thirty-eight states and the District of Columbia, however, still grant fault as well as no-fault divorces, and in those states proving fault can allow the damaged spouse to petition the court for a larger share of the property settlement.

Many lawyers will not do divorce work. One reason is that divorce cases can drag on forever. Years after the divorce is granted, one disgruntled spouse can haul the other into court to argue for more child support or visitation rights.

Another is the bitterness frequently accompanying divorce proceedings. Although there are some divorce attorneys who intentionally fan the flames of acrimony in their clients to drive up their own legal fees, many lawyers are repelled by the venting of emotions by their clients and avoid divorce work like the plague. I (D.G.) am one of those attorneys.

After handling one divorce case as a favor to a friend, I refused ever to do divorce work again. After working out a complex financial settlement between the divorcing couple, who were dividing up assets in the high six figures, the case reached an impasse when the two refused to agree on who would get the coffeemaker. After weeks of trying to convince my client, and of my opposing counsel trying to convince his, to compromise, I bought a coffeemaker and gave it to my client on the courthouse steps. When I thrust it into his hands and told him, "Here's your goddamn coffeemaker, now let's get this case over with," he finally saw the light. So did I.

It is unfortunate that the strong positive emotions that brought a couple together in the first place can be transformed into a nastiness just as intense. In such situations, combatants frequently forget where their best interests lie, and their primary motivation becomes vengeance to the point that they are prone to make self-destructive decisions.

There's an old Chinese custom called *majie*, which roughly translated means "to curse the street." When one family member gets mad at another, instead of venting anger and perhaps in the process fostering an atmosphere of hostility and hurt, the angered party will go outside and "curse the street." In a divorce case, in which anger threatens to displace objectivity, both parties might be wise to adopt the Eastern way and scream at a stop sign instead of each other.

## Doing It Yourself

If you have no children, few assets, and no major legal issues to work out, and you and your spouse have calmly and *amicably* agreed that it's time to pull the plug on your marriage, you can save considerable legal fees by purchasing one of the several do-it-yourself legal divorce kits available on the market. Forms are included and the two of you can fill them out and file them with the court according to instruction.

If your breakup is at least civil if not amicable, a consensual settlement agreement will in all likelihood stand without challenge by either party. Such an agreement is not inviolate, however, and can occasionally come back to haunt you. Years later, your ex can take you to court and claim that he or she didn't fully understand what he or she was signing away and petition for a piece of the action.

Say, for instance, you wrote a book while you were married, but were unable to get a publisher interested. Because you wrote it while you were married, it is legally community property (at least in community property states), but because it was a bust, your husband saw no reason to fight over the rights. Years later, the book is sold and you start to collect royalties, and suddenly your husband resurfaces and says he wants his share. You end up in court fighting the same battle you would have years before, with the same cost and heartache.

If you both decide to go it on your own, make a complete list of all your assets, including those which may currently be worthless, but which may some day have value. Discuss with your spouse openly which of those assets he is willing to waive claim to and which he is not, and include them in the settlement agreement.

If the terms of your settlement agreement have been amicably worked out and you wish to save on legal costs but are afraid you might have missed something in the drafting process, you might consider hiring a mutually-agreed-upon attorney to draw up the papers for you. Such an attorney should charge no more than $500 to $1,000 to take you through the process.

Because such an arrangement could later be challenged in that the attorney had an inherent conflict of interest representing both parties, the attorney will usually insist that he or she represent one of the parties—usually the wife—and that the husband state in writing that he is representing himself.

Saying all that, if you can work things out with your spouse and part without getting dueling attorneys involved, you will be way ahead in the game. The important thing during a gut-wrenching ordeal like divorce is to get on with your new life as quickly and painlessly as possible, not to prolong the pain with bickering and litigation.

## Mediation

Some couples seek to avoid an expensive legal battle by going to a divorce mediator. In some states, mediation is required by law before a couple takes their differences to court. In the rest of the states, mediation is a voluntary process in which the divorcing couple, with the aid of a disinterested third party, try to work out their differences and reach a consensual property settlement agreement.

Mediation can work if both parties are willing to be reasonable and fair. Mediators will help guide the discussion, cool the emotional atmosphere, and gather information about assets, liabilities, and debts. If one or both parties are emotional, intractable, or duplicitous (testimony during mediation generally is not given under oath; therefore the parties may lie), mediation will most likely be an exercise in futility.

Unfortunately, since the educational backgrounds of most mediators is in the social sciences, particularly psychological counseling, often they are woefully ignorant of complex financial issues, business and tax law, and accounting practices—all of which are often crucial in working out an equitable settlement for both sides. Therefore, mediation tends to work best when the couple have few or no assets to divide and really have no great issues to debate. Furthermore, since mediation agreements may not be legally enforceable unless later approved by the court, they can come under attack later by lawyers from one side or the other.

Some mediators are not professionally certified, but in some states they are required to be licensed (the qualifications for licensing vary from state to state). If your lawyer doesn't know of a qualified mediator, you can get names from the state bar or contact the Academy of Family Mediators, 1500 South Highway 100, Suite 355, Golden Valley, MN 55416, (612) 525-8670.

## Pre-Lawyer Arrangements

As soon as you have made your decision to divorce, there are certain things you should do to prepare yourself for your initial meeting with an attorney.

Go through your financial records carefully and completely, making a list of all assets and liabilities (debt is a communal responsibility, too), pensions, deferred profit sharing accounts, retirement benefits, and similar items. Separate out what was accumulated after you got married and what you came into the marriage with (although after ten years of marriage, courts tend to consider most assets commingled).

Talk to your financial adviser. He or she may recommend you put part of your assets in trust for your children or may have advice on what to do about your business if you have one.

During the process of negotiating a settlement, you will have to give up something, so determine early what is important to you and what is less important. If you have a business, for instance, you might want to protect it at the expense of another asset, like your share of the house. If custody of your children is your priority, you may be willing to make concessions to gain it. If you need a tax write-off, you might be willing to grant your wife more alimony in exchange for less child support, since alimony is deductible and child support is not. (Although in most states child support is set by formula according to your annual earnings, there is a range the court will allow.)

Having your goals in mind, as well as having all your legal papers and financial records organized before you meet with your lawyer, will save you considerable legal expense later on.

## Picking Your Attorney

Since divorce is often an agonizing process, it is important that you find an attorney who is not only trustworthy but emotionally supportive. If you have no clue whom to retain as your divorce attorney, a good place to go for a recommendation is a local men's or women's rights group.

### Whom to Retain

- Someone who has a reputation for honesty and whom you feel you can trust.
- Someone who is interested in you as a client and sympathetic to your situation.
- If your divorce involves complex financial issues, someone with a background in business who is well versed in property and tax law as well as estate planning.

- Someone whose practice is at least 50 percent divorce or family law. *Experience is crucial.*
- Someone who, while sympathetic, retains a calm demeanor. Emotion is your enemy in a divorce proceeding. You need an attorney who has your best interests at heart and who will help you keep your head while guiding you through rough waters.
- Someone not afraid to go to court. Although only 10 percent of divorce cases end up in court, the rest being resolved through settlement, your attorney must have had courtroom experience if your case gets to that point.

### Whom to Avoid

- Lawyers who advertise cut-rate divorces. Most of the time you get what you pay for—a divorce mill.
- Gender lawyers. Some male lawyers will only represent husbands and some female lawyers only wives. These attorneys often have a grudge to settle. They probably think they were wronged by the judicial system when they got their own divorces, and they get personal pleasure in carrying on their own vendettas against the opposite sex. These people will spend your money to attempt to right their own personal misfortune.
- Lawyers who aggressively fan the fires of your emotions. If a lawyer makes statements like "We're going to really sock it to him," "We're going to take him to the cleaners," or "He is asking too much as a settlement—didn't he already rip your guts out?" pick up your papers and leave. These lawyers love to litigate because they can collect enormous sums and eat up your assets in the process.
- Lawyers whose reputation for being difficult precedes them. If a friend recommends the attorney she retained for her divorce because the lawyer is a real "ball buster," ignore her. As illustrated in the beginning of this

chapter, by stubbornly refusing to compromise, whether by design or by their own nature, such lawyers serve only themselves, not their clients.

- Lawyers who are afraid to go to court. While you will want to avoid going to court if possible, you want to be in capable hands if you end up there. If the attorney tries to rush you into a quick settlement, it could be he has courtroom phobia. If he tells you you are being unreasonable in your demands or your refusal to give in to the opposition, weigh his counsel as objectively as you can. It might be his assessment is correct. It also might be that he just wants to settle your case and get on to the next payday.

### What to Ask

During the initial and subsequent meetings, certain important questions should be posed and answered by both you and your attorney. He or she should want to know about your financial situation, what led to the breakup of your marriage, what kind of a person your spouse is, whether your separation was hostile or friendly, whether you have children and how you want to deal with them, and what you are looking for in a settlement agreement. Answer all questions put to you by your attorney fully and truthfully; lies or intentional omissions will only come back to haunt you later.

You, on the other hand, will want to know what percentage of the lawyer's caseload is family law—in particular, divorce—and how many divorces he or she has handled over the past two years. If the answer is less than 30 percent, get yourself other counsel. Ask about courtroom experience: Your objective is to avoid court if possible, but if it's not possible, you'll need somebody at your side who can handle the job. If your case is going to involve complicated business transactions or the transfer of property, ask how experienced the lawyer is in the areas of tax and real estate law.

Although it has been pointed out elsewhere in this book, it bears repeating that you should hire a local attorney who has a good relationship with the judges who preside over the family law court. These attorneys are familiar with the judges' past rulings and can often accurately predict the outcome of your case. Their suggestions to the court are also as a general rule given weight by a judge familar with their expertise.

## Temporary Relief

Once you are locked into the legal process of divorce, the attorney for the dependent spouse—usually the wife—should make a motion for temporary relief, which is a court-stipulated amount to take care of her needs and the needs of the couple's children until a final judgment is rendered.

In many cases, however, the temporary relief isn't temporary. Often whatever a judge orders as temporary relief becomes permanent, as trial judges assume the previous judge had a rational basis for awarding the amount he did. Therefore, the wife's attorney should fight for as much temporary relief as he can get, and conversely, the husband's attorney should do everything he can to get the payments as low as possible. The husband should bring check stubs and any other pertinent financial information to court, *even if his attorney doesn't ask for them*, to show the judge what he is able to pay.

## Negotiation and Settlement

Settlement agreements deal with the disposition of the couple's assets and debts, and the scheduling of future payments. Assets are classified as marital or separate property. Payments will include spousal support and child support.

In the nine community property states (Arizona, California, Idaho, Louisiana, Nevada, New Mexico, Texas, Washington, and Wisconsin), any property owned by a person before the marriage remains his or her own, while any property acquired during the marriage is considered jointly owned, except money or property obtained during the marriage by bequest or gift. All other states use a formula of "equitable distribution" of assets, which takes into account such factors as the length of the marriage, the couple's style of living, and the spouses' skills and employability.

In setting spousal support, the earning or potential earning capacity of each party is considered. Spousal support used to be granted indefinitely, but most states now have formulas that grant support for only a fixed time based on a percentage of the length of the marriage, although the amount awarded can vary widely. In almost all jurisdictions, child support, within a range, will be set according to the income of the supporting spouse. A lawyer who tells you that you can be awarded or forced to pay an outlandish amount of child support does not know what he is talking about or is hoping you don't know what he is talking about.

Go into your settlement negotiations armed with as much information as possible. Try to find out what the normal range of such payments is in your county and state. Talk to some friends who have gone through divorces in your area and find out what they paid or received. Many courts have printed formulas for child support and spousal payments based on income and expenses. Find out if yours does. That way, when your lawyer tells you you've gotten the best possible deal, you will have something against which to judge his assessment.

During the settlement negotiations, both sides will be jockeying for position. If your lawyer is good, he will have a strategy based on what you have told him are your goals. Every concession by you should result in a concession by the other side. The more important your concession, the more important your spouse's concession should be. If your attorney is not achieving this, he is not doing his job.

## Negotiating Rules to Live By

- If you want something specific stipulated in the agreement, insist on it, provided it is reasonable.
- Don't let your attorney bully you into putting your name to an agreement you cannot live with.
- Insist everything be in writing. Don't fall for the "We've got the basic parameters down; the details will be worked out by the attorneys" line.
- *Read and understand everything before you sign.* Make sure what is on paper is what you agreed to orally. If you have questions, ask your attorney. That's what you're paying him for.
- During these sessions, always take your own notes, in as much detail as possible. Lawyers are fallible and miss things. If yours misses something important, you could end up getting shafted.
- If you have faith in your attorney and he tells you that you have the best deal you're going to get, consider taking his advice. Ask him the basis of his opinion. Go over with him what you've gained and what you've given away and weigh it against the goals you established at the beginning of the process. But remember, your lawyer isn't going to be living with your agreement, you are. In the end, the decision whether to sign on the dotted line has to be yours.

There is an old cliché in the law business that is probably a truism: If both sides to a settlement are unhappy, there is a good chance the agreement reached is fair and reasonable.

## Trial

If negotiations break down, you will end up where you don't want to be if you can avoid it—in court.

If your attorney is reluctant to try your case, ask why. If

his assessment of your situation is pessimistic and his reasoning is sound, you may want to reconsider and settle. But if you feel your lawyer is wrong or just plain scared (you'll probably know this by now, having had the opportunity to see him in action during pretrial courtroom proceedings), you might want to find another lawyer more inured to combat.

Get a second opinion by taking all of the details with you and paying the lawyer his hourly fee for an analysis. It is best if you can tell him that your present attorney knows you are getting a second opinion.

## The Never-Ending Story

Even after the settlement has been reached and your divorce is finalized by the court, your legal problems may not be over. Years later, if the circumstances of either party in a divorce radically alter, the cellophane can come off the can of worms. In almost all states, upon petition, child support payments may be increased in the interest of the child. Moreover, if the parent who is ordered to pay experiences a significant drop in income, he or she can ask the court to reduce the amount of support. In theory, children are entitled to have the same standard of living enjoyed by their parents. If the parent who is paying child support enjoys an increase in pay, child support can go up. Likewise, if the payer's income drops, so should child support payments, at least according to the law.

Notwithstanding this, in most jurisdictions, couples are allowed to stipulate in divorce agreements that the parties are prohibited from altering alimony awards in the future. Such clauses can be dangerous for both parties due to the possibility of changing financial fortunes.

# 12 Probate

Clayton Reynolds* didn't like to think about death, so he had always avoided making out a will. He also hated lawyers, a dislike that had grown out of the divorce of his first wife when the attorneys for both sides had walked off with roughly ten percent of the value of what he had managed to accumulate over the years. So when he decided to remarry and a friend suggested that he should draw up a will to make sure his estate was passed on to whom he wanted, Clayton decided to do the job himself.

From his first marriage of twenty-two years, Clayton had three children, two sons, Oscar and Clayton, Jr., and a daughter, Susan. Oscar had a successful job on an executive level with a major Fortune 500 company. Susan, Clayton's favorite, was married and had three children of her own, and although happy, was struggling to make ends meet. Clayton, Jr., had turned into a drug addict and after doing a short stint in prison for burglary, was disowned by his father, who would tell anyone that would listen that "Junior is no part of me. As far as I'm concerned, he's not my kid."

Clayton wrote out his will on his personal stationery, dated and signed it:

"I, Clayton Reynolds, upon my death, give my beloved daughter, Susan, all the money I have in the bank. I give my personal property to my son, Oscar. If I own any real estate at the time of my death, I want it split evenly between the children."

Clayton had intentionally left out of the will mention of his first wife, who had already gotten fifty percent of his assets, his drug addict son, Clayton, Jr., and his current wife, Gussie, not knowing how the new marriage would work out. He figured he could always change the will later, if he wished to provide for her. He thought he'd made a wise decision when, five months later, the marriage fell apart and Gussie moved out. He would never know how wrong that assumption was.

When Clayton dropped dead of a heart attack two months after his separation, his daughter Susan brought the one-page will to a lawyer. When he determined that there was $1 million in cash in banks and two pieces of real estate valued at $400,000, the lawyer enthusiastically agreed to handle the probate, expecting his fees would total $50,000. Papers were filed with the court, the children and both wives were given notice that Susan was applying for Letters of Administration, and a date was set in probate court for Susan to be appointed administrator of the estate.

Then it began.

Receiving her notice, Gussie went to her own lawyer, who immediately saw a big problem with the will and a big opportunity for Gussie and himself. Because Clayton had drawn up the will *before* the marriage, the document did not reflect the existence of the marriage or his wife and, according to state law, as a wife, Gussie was entitled to one-third of Clayton's separate property and *all* community property accumulated during their marriage. The lawyer offered to take on the case on a contingency basis, for fifty percent of what he recovered, and Gussie readily agreed, considering whatever she got to be found money.

Oscar took his notice to a lawyer friend who saw another big flaw in the will, in that, according to law, money is considered "personal property." By leaving Oscar his "personal property," Clayton had inadvertently bequeathed Oscar his bank account. Oscar's lawyer also was willing to work on a contingency basis.

Jennifer, Clayton's first wife, who as a result of the divorce had been awarded one-half of the accumulated property of the marriage, plus $10,000 a year alimony, went back to her old divorce lawyer who informed her that although alimony normally terminates upon the death of the payer, Clayton had been required as part of the settlement to maintain a $500,000 insurance policy with Jennifer as beneficiary, just in case of such an eventuality. Clayton, however, had let the policy lapse. Following her attorney's advice, Jennifer filed a $500,000 creditor claim against Clayton's estate.

Clayton, Jr., who was doing another stint in jail for parole violation, got in touch with his old court-appointed attorney who determined that Jr. was an "omitted heir," i.e., a son or daughter who is not mentioned in a will. In order to disinherit someone such as a son, who would inherit in the natural course of events, that son should be mentioned in the will and specifically disinherited. To make matters worse, Clayton had specified that his personal property be divided equally among "the children," not just the two named in the will. Clayton, Jr.'s lawyer agreed to go take the case on a fifty percent of recovery basis.

The outcome?

Since creditor claims take precedence over claims by heirs, Jennifer walked away with $500,000 off the top. Actually, she walked off with $400,000 and her lawyer walked off with $100,000.

Since they were married such a short time, Gussie and Clayton's community property was minimal, but as the omitted wife, she ended up with one-third of the remaining estate, or $300,000. For his diligent work, her attorney took his $150,000 fee.

The three children ended up splitting the remaining $600,000 evenly, less their respective attorneys' fees.

So, through good intentions and his effort to save on attorney's fees, Clayton managed to create a two-year legal battle, set family members against one another, and give $550,000 of his estate to attorneys.

Probate is a procedure which changes the legal ownership of your property when you die. During probate, the court determines whether your will is valid and also supervises the work of the executor or administrator of your estate, who is appointed by your will or, in some cases, the court.

The administrator "opens the estate" by filling out and filing the required forms with the court and by notifying all interested parties, such as relatives, heirs, and creditors, of the person's death. The administrator is also responsible for submitting to the court a detailed inventory of the decedent's real and personal property, as well as debts, within a legally specified time frame, usually one to six months. After a period of time to allow claims to be filed against the estate, the administrator pays off any taxes and administration costs and distributes the remaining assets to the decedent's heirs. After the administrator shows that all the proper notifications were made and expenses paid, a final accounting is filed with the court and the estate is "closed."

Although in reality probate is nothing more than a

transfer of title and usually involves little more than filling out and filing papers, the process can be laborious and can take from six months to a year to complete.

## Your Will

The cornerstone of any estate plan is a will, which is nothing more than a legal document that lays out how you wish your assets to be distributed upon your death, names your executor, and, if you wish, names a guardian to take care of your children.

If you die without a will, you die *intestate* and the state will divide your assets according to its law. Nearly every state has laws that differ from sister states, and while most provide for the surviving spouse and children, in other aspects there is a diversity of who will inherit. If you died intestate and wished a special bequest, however, such as leaving money to a friend or your favorite charity, you would be out of luck in all states.

Certain property is automatically excluded from your will, namely, community property from your marriage and property owned in joint tenancy with another person, as well as money which goes to beneficiaries already named by you, such as payments from life insurance policies, living trusts, and retirement accounts.

A will isn't a way to avoid probate. The court will make sure that your will is valid, appoint the executor named in your will, and supervise the executor's work to make sure he or she is performing according to your wishes.

What constitutes a legal will varies from state to state.

1. *Handwritten, or holographic, wills may be valid in certain jurisdictions if they meet certain standards*. Such wills must be legibly written, signed, and dated. Although it may not be necessary to have the will witnessed, it is always a good idea. It is *not* a good idea, however, for any beneficiary of a will

to act as a witness, as he or she may thereby be excluded from inheriting. Because of the lack of legal expertise possessed by the layperson, holographic wills can be full of pitfalls and susceptible to challenge, as was illustrated by the case of Clayton Reynolds in the beginning of this chapter. They are a feast for lawyers; therefore, we don't recommend them.

2. *Oral, or "deathbed," wills are not legal in some states*, and in those in which they are, the circumstances under which they are allowed are usually severely limited. In other words, it's not a good idea to wait until the last minute to orate your final wishes.

3. *Videotaped wills are not legally binding*, contrary to what you've seen in the movies in which Vincent Price appears on a TV screen to read his will to his heirs.

### Drawing Up Your Own Will

If you want to save yourself the expense of an attorney and have a fairly simple estate to distribute, you can draft your own will.

The primary elements any will should contain are:

1. A clause giving your full name and address and attesting that you are the author of the will.

2. A clause invalidating any previous wills.

3. A clause providing for the payment of taxes and debts.

4. A complete listing of your assets and how you want them distributed.

5. A clause naming your executor.

6. A common disaster clause as to how you wish your property to be distributed in the event you and your spouse die at the same time.

If you decide to draft your own will, keep in mind that you are running the risk of writing one that can be deemed by the court to be incomplete or unclear, and therefore invalid, as well as one that can be open to interpretation and challenged by disgruntled relatives.

There are numerous books on the market on how to write a will, as well as computer software programs such as Willmaker (DOS, Windows, and Macintosh), available from Nolo Press 950 Parker St., Berkley, CA 94710, for about $70. If you use such software, however, you will be limited to the options it provides.

In some states, fill-in-the-blanks wills are available from the state bar. California, for example, has two do-it-yourself form wills: a standard will and a will with trust. If your state bar has such forms, they can usually be ordered for a nominal sum and a self-addressed, stamped envelope.

It is our advice, however, not to draw up your own will, but to hire an attorney to do it. Our reasons are simple:

1. You retain flexibility in your will and can tailor it to fit your needs.

2. You can insure that your will is legally drafted, uses legally precise language, and is less susceptible to challenge.

Self-drafted wills are often filled with ambiguities which can end up being resolved only by expensive litigation. For instance, if a person provides in his will that he leaves his business to his son, what exactly does that mean? The business itself? The building in which the business is located? How about the land the building is on? Does it include accounts receivable and the cash in the business bank account? It may be perfectly clear to the author what he or she meant when drafting a will, but unclear to anyone else, and the testator is no longer around to explain.

3. You can get the lawyer's advice on estate planning, including the tax consequences of your decisions. This is especially important if your estate is complex—for example, involving a business or corporation.

4. There is such a thing as being penny-wise and pound-

foolish. Unless you have an estate of $500,000 or more, a lawyer should not charge more than $200 to $300 to draft your will. (If he or she tells you it will be more than that, go to another lawyer.) For a few hundred dollars, you can have the peace of mind that the job was done right. If the lawyer is going to be handling the probate of your estate, he or she might even draw up your will for only the cost of his or her overhead, knowing that the bigger payday is down the road.

## Probate

### Doing It Yourself

Some people seek to avoid legal fees by acting *in pro per*, that is, doing it themselves.

There are books on the market about how to negotiate the probate process without an attorney. But be warned: The process can be exacting and, at times, complicated. In California, for example, the Post Mortem Administration Checklist is forty-one pages long! Although it is basically a clerical job, consisting mostly of checking boxes on court forms, if you check the wrong box, you can get shafted.

Remember also: Most judges *hate* it when a person appears before them *in pro per*. That is because *in pro per* parties often seek advice and help in the courtroom and thus take up more of a judge's valuable time. I have seen judges who will go out of their way to slam-dunk *in pro per* parties by looking for flaws in their paperwork, thus invalidating the probate.

### Paralegals

If you insist on going through probate without an attorney, and the estate is a no-brainer, you may be well advised to hire a paralegal to help you through the process. In a majority of estates, there is little lawyering involved, and when a lawyer is hired, most of the work is frequently done by office paralegals anyway. While a paralegal cannot give you legal advice, for a fraction of what an attorney would charge he or she can help you fill out the forms correctly. If necessary, the paralegal can guide you toward a certified public accountant who is experienced in estate taxation.

### Hiring an Attorney

If the estate is complicated, or if you would feel more comfortable being led through the process, you will probably want to hire an attorney. Before you commit yourself, shop around. Look for an attorney who specializes in estate law. These attorneys are transactional attorneys, who have a solicitor mentality. Do not under any circumstances use a litigator to handle your probate. That particular breed of attorney is contentious by nature and could end up costing you plenty in the long run.

Many lawyers will tell you that their fees are set by law. Don't believe it. There is no law that says a lawyer can't take less than is allowed by state codes. The statutes set forth only the maximum that can be charged.

In some states, lawyers' fees are based on a percentage value of the estate. These percentages vary from state to state, but are usually computed on a sliding scale. In California, for example, attorneys' fees are set at 4 percent of the first $15,000 of the estate, 3 percent for up to $50,000, 2 percent of the next $850,000, and so on.

This system, crafted by lawyers for lawyers, was allegedly based on the assumption that the larger the estate, the more complicated will be the probate; therefore, the more time-consuming it will be for the attorney. The real reasoning behind it, however, was to insure that lawyers reaped the maximum amount in fees for the minimum amount of work. It takes exactly the same amount of paperwork to transfer ownership of $500,000 of stock as of $5,000, but for the same work, the attorney can reap a windfall!

Recognizing the inequity of percentage fees, some states have adopted probate codes based on "reasonable fees," that is, fees based on the amount of work the attorney actually puts into the case, and the amount of skill required to handle the work. A complicated tax case, for example, might require the skills of an attorney with special knowledge of tax law; therefore, the lawyer might be awarded an extra fee by the court.

The problem with "reasonable fees" is semantic. Judges, being lawyers themselves, are often very generous in determining what is reasonable and often rubber-stamp whatever fees the lawyers before them are asking.

In addition, a lawyer can petition the court for *extraordinary fees*, or ex-o's as they're known in the trade, for services rendered out of the ordinary. For instance, if a property is sold off during probate and the sale is contested by a creditor, or if the validity of the will is challenged by a disgruntled heir, the probate procedure becomes more complicated than merely filing papers and the appeal process can take up more of the lawyer's time than anticipated. Ex-o's are paid out of the estate.

Probate lawyers look for any occurrence, procedure, or event they can use to justify ex-o's. Before ex-o's are granted, a hearing must be held during which the attorney makes his request. Beneficiaries of the estate must be notified and can attend the hearing and object if they feel the fees petitioned for are out of line.

There are several ways to keep your probate lawyer's fees down.

- Find out if the probate can be handled nonjudicially. Many state probate codes permit non-court-supervised probate.

- Ask the lawyer to cap his fees. The lawyer may be willing to do that, particularly if the estate is a large one.
- Look for an attorney who will work by the hour instead of on a percentage basis. That way, the attorney will be paid only for the time he or she actually puts into your case.
- Get a written agreement with the lawyer specifying what fees will be paid, what the basis of the fees will be, and that the lawyer will be paid only on an hourly basis for work done. Also try to get the attorney's estimate of fees on paper as well as an agreement to submit itemized bills to you.
- If the attorney is willing to give you an estimate of his fees to complete probate, but is unwilling to cap his fees, ask to be kept informed as fees approach the lawyer's outside estimate. Then get an explanation as to why fees are running higher than expected.
- Reduce the lawyer's workload by using him or her only for consultation purposes. If you are the executor or administrator, you will be doing most of the work, such as inventorying assets, determining debts, taking care of property, and arranging a sale or rental of real estate.
- Before hiring an attorney, carefully look over the estate assets and debts and try to identify what snags might be encountered and what challenges issued against the estate. Inform the attorney of possible problems and ask for an estimate of *all* costs, including ex-o's, that would be necessary to handle them. Ask the attorney if he can see any possible irregularities that you can't, and if he can, ask what the ballpark figure would be to settle them.
- If the attorney's fees are based on a percentage of the estate, make sure the fees are based on the net value of the *probate estate*, not the gross estate. The probate

estate is the total assets distributed by the administrator, less taxes paid before the estate is closed and those assets inherited outside the probate, such as insurance policies, and individual retirement accounts. It is not uncommon for a slick attorney to try to jack up his fees by basing them on the gross estate, that is, the value of everything the deceased owned at death. For example, if the estate has in it an apartment building worth $400,000 which has a mortgage of $250,000, the equity is $150,000, a substantial difference in fees. Don't let the attorney get away with it.

- If the attorney who drafted the decedent's will names himself the executor, make sure he or she does not collect *both* fees. Because courts in some states frown on this practice, one way some greedy attorneys try to circumvent the issue is to use the "buddy system." Through arrangement with a "buddy" lawyer, the executor-attorney hires the "buddy" to represent him as legal counsel through the probate. The "buddy," in turn, will reciprocate and hire the original attorney whenever he, the "buddy," is named executor of an estate. If you suspect some sort of arrangement like this is at work, you should file a *timely* objection with the court. The reason we stress "timely" is that if you don't raise the objection when you first receive notice that the executor has hired an attorney, you may be too late.

In most states, estate administrators are allowed to collect an amount from the estate for services rendered. Often, the maximum allowed by law is the same percentage as that allowed for the estate's attorney. Thus, the attorney would collect 3 percent on the first $50,000 and the administrator would also be able to collect 3 percent. Notwithstanding what was said above, in some states it is perfectly legal for the lawyer, when acting as the administrator, to collect both amounts. But while the law may allow for that eventuality, it does not mean that the attorney can't waive the administrator's fee. Make sure up front that he or she is willing to do just that.

## Appeal of Fees

If you feel the request for fees by the estate lawyer or administrator is out of line, you can petition the probate court for a reduction. Requirements for such petitions vary from state to state, but generally the request must be filed with the court within thirty to sixty days before the notice of approval of the final accounting and the decree of final distribution. The estate cannot be closed and assets cannot be distributed until the court rules on the petition.

Many times, such petitions fall on deaf ears. Judges have a tendency to be sympathetic to lawyers, especially when the rule of reasonableness is so vague as to be almost meaningless. Occasionally, however, a petitioner's request for a reduction is granted, especially if it can be proven that the fees requested are totally out of whack with the time and labor the lawyer expended. So keep that log of the lawyer's time as complete as possible.

Make the lawyer produce a time sheet showing time actually spent on the matter. Check that two or three lawyers did not appear in court at the same time if the matter did not warrant it. For extraordinary fees, lawyers will make court appearances when not necessary. The fact of the matter is that many, if not most, probate matters are capable of being handled over the phone with a probate examiner.

Probate examiners are civil service employees employed by the court. Often they are attorneys highly skilled at probate. The examiner's job is to analyze every probate file before it goes to the judge. If everything is in conformity with the probate codes and there are no unusual circumstances to the case, the examiner will stamp "Recommend approval" and pass the matter on to the judge, who will in all likelihood approve the petition as recommended. If there is a protest in court by an heir, the matter will be set aside for future consideration.

It is often not necessary for an attorney to appear in court to determine whether or not a petition has been recommended for approval by a probate examiner. All the attorney has to do is call up the examiner or the court to determine if approval is recommended. If you have some question about the size of your probate lawyer's bill, go to the court and pull your file. Most of the time, the probate examiner's notes will be in the file, showing if he or she recommended approval of your case. If it shows that the examiner indeed recommended approval and your attorney billed you for unnecessary court appearances, you should ask him why the appearances were justified. If his/her answer is unsatisfactory, protest.

## Living Trusts

Many people think they can avoid attorney's fees and the costs and hassles of probate by setting up a living trust. That may or may not be true.

In essence, a living trust is just that. You are creating a legal entity to which you entrust your assets and possessions for safekeeping while you are alive. In doing so, you must choose a trustee, an entity or person to administer the trust upon your death.

There are two major types of living trusts: *revocable* and *irrevocable*.

A *revocable living trust* allows you to change its provisions while you are alive. As your own trustee, you retain control over your assets and circumvent the costs and time involved in probate upon your death. The trust agreement becomes fixed in concrete at the time of your death, when the trustee or trustees you appoint take over your assets.

When the new trustees take over, they are required to follow the instructions set out in the document. First, they must pay all just debts and federal and state estate taxes. Inheritance taxes vary from state to state and also change depending on the relationship between the beneficiary and decedent. A surviving spouse, for example, is exempt from federal estate tax and many states' taxes. This leaves children and other beneficiaries to pick up most of the tab. Thus, the living trust does not eliminate taxes, but does avoid court costs and attorney's fees that go along with probate.

When you set up an *irrevocable living trust*, you relinquish all ownership of the property you put in trust. An irrevocable trust can be used as an estate planning tool and, if set up wisely, can result in savings in estate taxes. The downside is that the grantor (the creator of the trust) can't change the terms of the trust, and in some cases the grantor cannot receive income from the trust while he or she is alive. Irrevocable trusts can be very complex and should be carefully planned with the aid of a good estate attorney. By doing this, you retain all of the rights of an owner of your property and, upon your death, title is automatically transferred to those whom you want to receive it.

Another, more dangerous, method to avoid probate is to create a joint tenancy wherein the surviving tenant takes title to the property immediately upon the death of the co-tenant. If a husband and wife are joint tenants in a home, for example, or have joint checking accounts or hold stocks in both names, no probate is required for that property. Sometimes, in order to avoid attorney's fees and probate costs, a widow or widower will name a most trusted child as joint tenant on bank accounts, real estate, etc. We say this method is more dangerous because it is based totally on trust and money has the tendency to "cancel all relationships," as Karl Marx once said. You are trusting that joint tenant to distribute your assets as you desire, because there is no legal

remedy for brothers or sisters to collect the share you intended if the surviving tenant says, "Tough, it's all mine." If
your trust is misplaced, this method of avoiding probate can
be more costly in the long run, involving much litigation and
even the destruction of a family.

In general, the fewer assets you have, the less a trust will do
for you. For example, if you are a widow or widower with one or
more descendants and your assets consist of a house and a
small checking account, consider creating a life estate by
deeding the property to your intended beneficiaries and retain-
ing a life tenancy. Contact your banker and add the name of
your most trustworthy child as a joint tenant on the checking
account. Then make certain you advise all the intended
beneficiaries of how you want the savings to be divided.

In the newspapers, ads frequently publicize free seminars
on living trusts given by attorneys. At these seminars, the
attorneys look to solicit clients, often by offering to grind out
trust agreements at very low prices. The reason they price
their services so competitively is that they expect return
business that will generate big fees.

Here is how it works: At the seminars and later in the
lawyer's office, details of the trust are explained in simple
terms to the client. No instructions are given to the trustee
who will assume control of the assets at the time of the
trustor's death, however. The new trustee, realizing he or she
has now assumed some new and strange responsibilities, will
quite naturally seek the advice of a lawyer. Whom better to
consult than the attorney who prepared the document and
whose name, address, and telephone number are prominently
embossed on the instrument?

At the first meeting between the attorney and new client,
the seemingly simple living trust becomes very complex as
the duties of the trustee are explained. The lawyer will
emphasize the pitfalls and the liability that may result from
not filing documents properly or paying taxes in a timely

manner and how some of the beneficiaries might file a lawsuit if investments go sour. "Not to worry," the lawyer assures his new client. "I'll take care of everything and it won't cost you anything."

What isn't said is that the attorney's fees will be paid out of the trust estate and that if the new trustee is the beneficiary, his share of the inheritance will be duly diminished. In some cases, the loss can be quite serious, as in most states there are no statutes limiting such fees.

Whether a living trust is advantageous for you is a matter for you to decide. But it will cost you some money to consult with an attorney to find out. The only certainty is that the attorneys will get it from you when you are alive and they'll get it from you after you are dead.

# 13 Real Estate

When twenty-four-year-old secretary Rose Pucci found a three-room condo in the Beacon Hill section of Boston, she thought her dream had come true. She'd finally found a home of her own that she could afford on her $23,000 salary.

The reason the $45,000 condo was going so cheap was because it was under rent control and at the time was occupied by a belligerent tenant who didn't show any inclination toward moving. But because Boston's rent control ordinance clearly allowed an owner who wished to occupy a dwelling to take possession of it, she felt she was safe in investing her life savings in the property. Only she wasn't.

After assuming title and filing for eviction of the tenant, she found that the tenant had plans not only not to move, but also not to pay rent, in the hope of forcing a sale at a cut-rate price to himself. This "tenant from hell," as Ms. Pucci came to call him, knew how to play all the legal angles. How? Because he was a *lawyer*.

Ms. Pucci, outmatched and desperate for legal help, looked for a lawyer, but none would take her case on the installment plan. She applied for legal aid, but because her income was above the poverty level, she was turned down. She could not find any tenant–landlord consumer groups that helped landlords. Pucci found herself being eaten alive by mortgage payments and condo fees to the point that she could not afford even rent for herself. In the end, she became virtually homeless, living in her brother's apartment, her dreams shattered by the legal system.

The irony of the Pucci case is that in a vast majority of real estate transactions, the services of a lawyer are not needed, but in many states are foisted on the customer *as a matter of law*, courtesy of lawyer-dominated legislatures and lobbyists. But when Ms. Pucci *really* needed an attorney, she couldn't find one with enough compassion or trust to take her case, demonstrating that lawyers are like cops: When you're in dire need of one, they're nowhere to be found; when you don't need one, there's one on every corner.

These are real estate transactions in which you need the services of an attorney:

- You have purchased a home or other major piece of property and you find the seller has been dishonest in disclosing defects in the building, such as environmental hazards.
- The lender on your property begins a foreclosure proceeding against you or a creditor files a lien on your property for nonpayment of a debt. (A lien guarantees payment of the debt and can result at worst in the forced sale of your property.)
- You are involved in a very complex real estate deal, such as the sale or leasing of industrial or commercial property, and there is going to be development which

may involve municipal approvals or zoning and permit problems.

- You are a party to an unsolvable landlord–tenant dispute. (This will be dealt with in more detail later in the chapter.)
- Your transaction involves insurance issues or claims.
- You are suing or being sued for breach of contract.

Most other "vanilla" real estate transactions would not normally require attorney intervention if it were not for state laws demanding it.

## Buying a House

Buying a house can be the most expensive purchase the average person makes in his or her lifetime, which is why many safeguards have been put in place by law to protect the unwary consumer. It is also the rationale for getting lawyers involved.

The process in most states goes something like this: Once you have found the home you want to buy at a price you are willing to pay, you make a deposit (called *earnest money*) to demonstrate to the seller the seriousness of your intent. This deposit goes toward the down payment, and with it you submit a written offer. Often this is a preprinted form called the *deposit receipt*.

Once the deposit receipt is accepted by the seller, a binding contract is in place between you. In the contract should be all the terms of the deal: the sale price, the amount of the down payment, the terms of payment, and exactly what comes with the house. There should also be stipulations as to what conditions may allow you to get out of the contract—for instance, if an inspection shows a serious defect in the home. (Most states have stringent requirements compelling the seller to disclose visual [patent] and unseen [latent] defects in the property.) You may also want to stipulate that you can break the contract if you cannot get a loan or if you are unable to sell the house you currently own before buying the new one. If you make an offer and it is accepted by the seller, you cannot get out of the contract because you've found another house you like better or because you simply got cold feet thinking about the payments. Under those scenarios, the seller is entitled to keep your deposit.

After the terms are agreed upon and your financing is arranged with a lending institution, the buyer and seller enter into a final settlement agreement called a *title closing* or *escrow*. This involves the final signing of documents and disclosures mandated by the U.S. Department of Housing and Urban Development (HUD) and the transfer of funds from the buyer to the seller.

That is the skeletal process that takes place between the buyer and seller. But in *all* real estate transactions, there are other people who get into the act.

Most real estate transactions involve the employment of a real estate broker—usually two, one for the buyer, one for the seller. All states have laws and regulations spelling out the minimum education and experience needed to obtain a broker's license. Both real estate brokers are paid a commission by the seller.

By and large, real estate brokers today are well-trained professionals who will protect the interests of the parties they represent, although buyers must remember that because the broker is being paid a commission, it is in his or her interest to keep the sale price up.

After an agreement to purchase has been signed, a broker will obtain a preliminary title search by "opening an order" with a title insurance company. The title company will search the public records to make sure that the title on the property is "clear," that is, is free from easements, taxes, judgments, or claims against the property by creditors. Most lenders require that the buyer obtain title insurance before they will fork over money for a loan. There are different kinds of title insurance, and it can be paid for by either the buyer or the seller.

In a dozen or so states, escrow companies may legally handle real estate and loan transactions. These companies are neutral stakeholders that represent neither the buyer nor the seller; they owe a fiduciary duty—a duty of confidence and trust to the client—to both. They are closely regulated and regularly audited by state agencies. They have to post large fidelity and indemnity bonds that effectively guarantee buyers and sellers that the instructions given them will be followed and that none of their employees will embezzle the proceeds.

Escrow instructions are generally prepared from the sales deposit receipt and oral information provided by the principals or the brokers. Once these documents have been signed and the deposit given the broker received, an escrow officer will deal with the title company, make sure all the proper documents are in order, and arrange for the transfer of money and title.

In nonescrow states, the same procedure is followed, except that lawyers substitute for the escrow company. In these states, both the buyer and the seller must be represented by an attorney, thus assuring that the rights of both will be protected and double fees will be paid.

The real estate broker or the principals (in case the deal is a direct buyer-seller arrangement and a broker is not used) bring the sales contract to a title company. It prepares formal instructions and does everything an escrow company would have done except that, in addition, it sends copies of all documents to the lawyer representing the buyer and the one representing the seller. These lawyers then review the papers and affix their names approving the articles, and the deal closes. Typically, the lawyers doing this document "review" charge two to three times as much as escrow fees for transactions of comparable purchase price.

## Whom to Pick

If your transaction is a simple house sale or purchase and an attorney is foisted on you by law, it is best and least expensive to go to a law firm or lawyer who handles a high volume of such cases. Unlike personal injury mills, which are to be avoided at all costs, real estate mills are fine. The reason for this is that the transaction is usually simple and clean and can be handled with a minimum of the lawyer's time. A firm that does not have a production line in place for a run-of-the-mill house sale can rack up ridiculous billable hours. Lawyers in such a firm might intentionally or through inexperience make changes on the documents that will not be acceptable to the insurance company issuing the title insurance policy, requiring more changes and therefore higher legal fees.

One place to find a lawyer experienced in real estate transactions is to call a title company. Its employees will probably tell you they are not allowed to recommend lawyers, but they will likely be willing to give you half a dozen names of lawyers who do nothing but real estate work.

Similarly, your real estate broker will in all likelihood have the names of several lawyers with whom he or she has had dealings in the past. These recommendations are usually quite reliable: first because the agent will want a lawyer involved who will close the deal so he can collect his commission, and second because the agent is looking for repeat business and referrals and will not want you to feel ripped off.

After you get your half dozen names, call all the lawyers and explain briefly the type of transaction you want handled and the selling price. Ask each for his or her charges. Try offering less than they quote. Tell them that you know the price of the property has nothing to do with the amount of legal work involved (a $50,000 sale involves the same paperwork as a $500,000 sale). Once you have chosen the lawyer and agreed on the fee, ask the lawyer if he will be getting a commission from the title company he recommends and if you will be credited with that amount. Some lawyers double-dip by taking fees from both client and title company, driving up the cost of the title insurance policy. There's no reason you should pay the lawyer twice; let him know that.

If you live in an escrow state but feel insecure or intimidated by the process of buying a house, you probably should hire an attorney for your own peace of mind to go over the documents before you sign. A lawyer can answer your tax questions and advise you of your legal rights and responsibilities. In escrow states, you have another source—the escrow company—to guide you to an experienced real estate attorney.

## Landlord–Tenant Disputes

If you happen to own rental property, from time to time problems may arise with your tenants, including nonpayment of rent, damage to your property, or nuisances created by the tenant such as throwing wild parties.

If these problems cannot be resolved by rational conversation, you will probably need an attorney, due to the technicalities of the law governing such situations. It used to be that the landlord was king, but in recent years the law has strongly protected the tenant. For example, in California, until several years ago a landlord could sue in small claims court without the services of an attorney to evict a nonpaying tenant. The state court of appeals determined, however, that allowing a landlord to circumvent the services of the legal profession somehow violated deadbeat tenants' right to due process.

To evict a tenant, it is necessary to file an "unlawful detainer" action, or UD. Most UDs are quick legal procedures that take precedence over most other civil matters, due to the fact that damages can rapidly accrue by the occupancy of property without the payment of rent and because of the general inability in such a case to collect a money judgment. Because of the speed of this procedure, safeguards have been instituted to protect a tenant from an unreasonable and avaricious landlord. If one procedural error is committed, the landlord has to start the proceeding over from scratch.

If you are a landlord and have such a problem, you need a lawyer skilled in avoiding technical pitfalls. But be careful when choosing a UD attorney. Many who specialize in UDs have the various standard forms computerized, along with electronic tracking of the dates by which each step of the eviction process must be completed. Although a general practitioner can handle these matters, important deadlines might be missed or crucial steps omitted, resulting in a return to the starting line.

You can locate a UD lawyer through apartment house associations; property management companies, or real estate brokers; or by going to the courthouse and spending some time in the department that handles landlord–tenant matters. If you see a lawyer with three or four UDs on the calendar and the judge doesn't give him a bad time, he's your guy.

If you are a tenant who is being harassed by a landlord and you need a lawyer, avoid all the above sources except the latter. At the courthouse, watch for a lawyer representing tenant interests. Some other sources are legal aid (if you are too poor to afford an attorney), your local bar association, consumer organizations, and the municipal rent control board if your city has rent control.

If you have a serious dispute with your landlord but want to avoid litigation, you might see if the owner would be willing to try mediation. The process of finding a mediator has already been outlined in chapter 5.

## Keeping Costs Down

The main thing to remember in controlling legal costs in real estate matters is: *Be proactive.* Try to avoid the need for legal services by doing your homework up front. This will also help you keep your costs down later should you need an attorney, as well as bolster the likelihood of a favorable disposition in your case.

- Read all contracts and agreements thoroughly and ask questions as they arise, preferably in writing. If, for example, you are buying a condominium, ask the seller for a copy of the homeowners' association bylaws, the condo's financial statements, and documents that might reveal any unpaid assessments. Ask to see the minutes of the board association meetings to determine if there are any outstanding lawsuits that might affect the value of your purchase.

   If you are entering into a rental agreement, read it carefully and determine if there are any references to any other documents, such as "House Rules." Read any such documents and make any changes that the owner will agree to *before you sign.* If you want a longer notice period before the owner can raise your rent, for example, bring it up.

- Be an informed consumer. Know your rights and responsibilities.

- Leave a paper trail. This will save you many headaches later if the matter ends up in a dispute. For example, if you are purchasing a house and want information that is not in the owner's disclosure statement, which is supposed to list all defective features and structural defects, put your questions down on paper and ask the seller for answers in writing.

- If you are having work done on your home or are building your own home, look for a building contractor with a good reputation who is financially sound. If a contractor goes belly-up in the middle of building your house, you can be out a lot of money.

These are just a few examples of situations in which legal problems can be avoided or mitigated by expending a little effort in educating yourself and using that education. As the old adage goes: The best *defense* is good *offense*.

Rose Pucci might have saved herself a truckload of grief by thoroughly reviewing the rent control regulations that applied to the condo she was considering purchasing and determining what her remedies would be if the tenant decided to fight her attempt to evict, as he later did. She could also have interviewed neighbors and people with whom the attorney had business dealings, even interview the attorney himself to gauge the man's temperament and demeanor. Her research might have possibly raised some red flags and she might have decided not to buy, or at least she might have been able to have a strategy in place to counter the moves of the "tenant from hell."

# Conclusion: An Attitude Checklist

It is unfortunate that we live in a society in which the law has come to pervade almost every aspect of our lives, to the point that it is likely that every one of us will probably need the services of an attorney at least once in his or her lifetime.

Americans are increasingly viewing the legal system as a way to solve every personal, social, and economic problem. In this "claim and blame" society, we have come to believe that everything has a legal remedy, that somehow "total justice" can be achieved as long as somebody can be made to pay. The problem is we are all being made to pay, in and out of the courtroom, in social, economic, and personal costs. The only real winners in the game are the lawyers.

Among those traits Mary Anne Glendon finds in the best lawyers are an eye for the issue; a feeling for the common ground; an ability to foresee the future; a mastery of the law; an ability to problem solve; an ability to empathize with the client's problem, but still remain objective; and an ability to see other people's viewpoints. She goes on to say that "the more fully a lawyer excels in [these traits], the less likely it is that his or her work will receive acclaim beyond the circle of those immediately benefited. Peacemaking, problem-solving lawyers are the legal profession's equivalent of doctors who practice preventive medicine. Their efforts are generally overshadowed by the heroics of surgeons and litigators."

Even if you are lucky enough to find an attorney with all or some of those good traits described above, however, you still need to maintain a vigilant attitude in your dealings with him or her if you want to come through the relationship semi-whole. You will want to keep the following points in mind:

1. *Know what you want to accomplish and keep your goals realistic.*

2. *Take the time to evaluate your needs and carefully pick the attorney who will best get the job done.*

3. *Keep control of the situation.* You will have to live with your decisions for the rest of your life. Your lawyer will be on to his or her next case next week. Make sure your lawyer knows he or she is working *for you,* not the other way around.

4. *Stay involved with your case.* Constantly assess the results of your lawyer's actions and monitor his or her success.

5. *View your case as you would a business decision.* What is the likelihood of success or failure? Will success cost you more than it is is worth? If so, you might be advised to pack it in.

6. *Constantly monitor your lawyer's bills as they come in.* If you feel you have been overcharged, let the lawyer know it *before* you pay. Just because a lawyer hands you a bill does not mean it is etched in stone.

7. *Think more in terms of prevention and problem solving* than in getting involved in expensive and counterproductive litigation.

In an increasingly complex and litigious society, the layperson is at a distinct disadvantage. As Emory Cohen, corporate president of Laser-Pacific, puts it: "If you find you can't necessarily trust your lawyer, where are you?"

The answer must be: You are where you put yourself. There are ways to play the game to at least mitigate the hurt and to achieve the goals you desire.

# APPENDIXES

# APPENDIX A
# Attorney's Contract

**LAW OFFICES OF**
William Shakespeare

June 13, 1994

Mr. Joe Blow
646 No Such Road
Palm Springs, CA 92264-8404

Re: Retainer Agreement

Dear Mr. Blow:

Thank you for engaging this office relative to representing you in connection with Palm Springs B & S, Inc., a California corporation, ADF, a California general partnership, and John Kneejerk. You and I have worked together toward the hand service today of the demand correspondence to John Kneejerk, which we jointly determined may accomplish the result of making Tom Kneejerk negotiate fairly to acquire your interests in the partnership and the corporation, in order to avoid a dissolution action for the partnership and corporation.

As you know, the letter will be hand served on John Kneejerk at home and office today. Time will tell whether it will have the desired result on him, which is to avoid the necessity of suing him. However, if necessary, I am prepared to file corporate and partnership dissolution actions and to carry those matters all the way to trial with an eye toward achieving your desired result, which is maximizing to the fullest extent, on the most reasonable cost basis, the liquidation of your interests in the corporation and the partnership.

I know that you are aware of this law firm by reference of Tom Mouthpiece, and appreciate his referral of you to this office. I will endeavor to provide to you the level of service which will justify Tom's confidence in me by making of the referral.

Accordingly, as required by the Rules of Professional Responsibility requiring written fee agreements between attorneys and their clients, this letter is intended to serve to memorialize our Fee Agreement ("Contract"), orally entered into effective the 28th day of April, 1994, the date of our initial conference, by and between Joe Blow ("Client"), and the Law Offices of <u>William Shakespeare</u> ("Attorney").

1. <u>Scope of Agreement</u>. Client hires Attorney to provide legal services to Client in connection with your matter, above referenced.

2. <u>Duties of Attorney and Client</u>. Attorney shall provide those legal services reasonably required to represent Client in the matter described in paragraph 1 of this Contract. Attorney shall also take reasonable steps to keep Client informed of significant developments and to respond to Client's inquiries.

Client shall be truthful with Attorney, cooperate with Attorney, keep Attorney informed of developments, perform the obligations it has agreed to perform under this Contract, pay Attorney's bills in a timely manner, and keep Attorney apprised of its address, telephone numbers and whereabouts.

3. <u>Billing Rates</u>. As I explained, my normal billing rate is $225.00 per hour. However, I have offered to accept, and you agreed to pay for legal services at the rate of $200.00 per hour for all time spent on your case file. I will also bill for associated attorneys at rates of $135.00 to $185.00 per hour for all time spent on your case file, in the event of litigation. Time spent by law clerks will be billed at $75.00 per hour, and time spent by paralegals at $75.00 per hour. This hourly rate may change from time to time, typically in January and July of each year, upon the giving of notice to Client. However, these rates will not change to you prior to January 1, 1995, in any event. My policy is to provide the requisite talent and experience necessary for performance of each task to be performed by allowing the person with the lowest rate, capable of performing said task, to do so. No set amount of fees and/or costs has been quoted.

4. <u>Costs and Expenses</u>. Client shall reimburse Attorney for all actual costs and expenses incurred by Attorney, as necessary in the reasonable opinion of Attorney. Client authorizes Attorney to incur all reasonable costs in the handling of Client's matter.

5. <u>Statements</u>. Attorney shall send Client a statement for fees and costs incurred periodically. The timing of such periodic billings, however, shall be at the discretion of Attorney, and failure to provide billings monthly, or regularly shall not prejudice Attorney's right to collect for the same.

Client shall pay, when possible, Attorney's billing statements within thirty (30) days after the presentation of such billing statements. Unpaid sums shall bear interest at the rate of ten percent per annum, after thirty (30) days, and if collection activity becomes necessary, the prevailing party shall be entitled to reasonable attorneys fees and costs. However, you have indicated to me that you presently have cash flow problems, so I have agreed to work out delayed payment of your account, which I am certainly willing to do as cash flow reasonably permits.

If Attorney is at any time holding a deposit from Client, such Attorney's statement shall indicate what portion of the sums due has been paid out of the deposit, and what portion, if any, is then due and owing from Client to Attorney. Attorney reserves the right at any time, in his sole discretion to request additional amounts of advance retainer.

6. _Disclaimer_. Attorney has made no promises or guarantees to Client about the outcome of Client's matter, and nothing in this Contract shall be construed as such a promise or guarantee.

7. _Discharge and Withdrawal_. Client may discharge Attorney at any time, and Attorney may withdraw only for good cause. Among the facts constituting good cause are Client's breach of this Contract, Client's refusal to cooperate with Attorney or to follow Attorney's advice on a material matter, or any fact or circumstance that would render Attorney's continuing representation of Client unlawful or unethical. In such event, Attorney and Client each agree to sign any documents reasonably necessary to complete Attorney's discharge or withdrawal, including but not necessarily limited to Substitution of Attorney.

8. _Termination or conclusion_. Upon the termination or conclusion of Attorney's services, all unpaid charges for services rendered and costs incurred or advanced through the termination or conclusion date shall become immediately due and payable. Attorney acknowledges his obligation, upon Client's demand, to deliver Client's file to Client at or after the termination or conclusion of Attorney's services.

9. _Deposit_. Client has paid an initial retainer to Attorney on the date of our initial conference in the amount of $1,000.00. Said retainer shall apply toward Attorney's fees and costs thereafter incurred. Attorney will use the advanced retainer as payment against Attorney's fees, costs and expenses incurred, on a first in, first out basis. Any unused portion of this retainer at the conclusion of Attorney's services will be refunded to Client. Said amount is not held in trust, but is

deposited to Attorney's general account, and Client is entitled to no interest thereon.

10. Insurance. Law Offices of William Shakespeare carries legal malpractice insurance in amounts in excess of that required by law. This information is provided to you in accordance with the Rules of Professional Responsibility for attorneys in the state of California.

11. Commencement of Services. Execution signifies your concurrence that representation under this Agreement commenced upon our initial office conference on April 28, 1994. I look forward to serving your legal needs.

Please sign and retain one original of this Contract for your own records, sign the enclosed original of this Contract for my records. I will do my utmost to provide you the level of service and representation to justify your confidence in choosing this firm.

Sincerely yours,
LAW OFFICES OF William Shakespeare

By _William Shakespeare_
                William Shakespeare

Agreed to and accepted upon the above terms and conditions. I acknowledge receipt of a copy of this Contract.

"Client"

By _Joe Blow_
                Joe Blow

# Fee Agreement for Criminal Attorney

**MOUTHPIECE & MOUTHPIECE**
**ATTORNEYS AT LAW**
**COURTHOUSE BUILDING**
**FOURTH FLOOR**

FEE AGREEMENT

This FEE AGREEMENT covers the following matter:

_____.

1. The Municipal Court Retainer in this matter is $ _____.
The Superior Court Retainer in this matter is $ _____.
A Retainer reserves the time of the attorney for this particular case. A Retainer becomes the property of the attorney, regardless of the outcome of the case. For example, if the attorney stops prosecution of a case before filing, if the attorney settles a case in one Court appearance, or if the attorney is removed by the client from the case, the Retainer fee is earned and remains the property of the attorney.

2. The attorney reserves the right to modify or cancel the Fee Agreement in the event the charges are more serious then represented or if there are prior convictions and/or special allegations which are not disclosed, known, or anticipated. The Fee Agreement covers the matters written on this form.

3. The Preliminary Hearing fee is $ _____. This fee covers only the Municipal Court Hearings on the felony. Superior Court will be an additional and separate fee of $ _____.

4. Trials and Motions are billed at the rate of $ _____ per day. Part of a day is considered a full day.

5. Costs of suit (investigator, chemist, transcripts, expert witnesses, etc. ...) are the responsibility of the client and are not included in the attorney fee.

6. Department of Motor Vehicle Hearings are separate and distinct from Court procedures. DMV Hearings are $ _____.

7. The fee does not include Appeals, Writs or Re-Trials.

193

8. An associate attorney of JEFFREY GRAY may appear on your case at no additional cost.

9. No guarantee or representation as to the outcome of the case has been made.

10. Our office has liability insurance.

11. I have read, discussed, and understand this FEE AGREEMENT. I have received a copy of this FEE AGREEMENT.


DATED: _____        _____

                                                      CLIENT

                                       _____

                                                     ATTORNEY

# APPENDIX C
## Sample Legal Bill

**LAW OFFICES OF William Shakespeare**
745 Legal Drive
Palm Springs, CA 92262

August 12, 1994

Mr. Joe Blow
646 No Such Road
Palm Springs, CA 92264-8404

STATEMENT FOR PROFESSIONAL SERVICES

Client Matters: Palm Springs B & S, Inc.
ADF, a general partnership

| | Work Performed: | Hrs/Rate | Amount |
|---|---|---|---|
| 04/26/94 | Read and review documents faxed to office by client before conference with Joe Blow re B & S, Inc. and ADF. | 0.50 200.00/hr | 100.00 |
| 04/28/94 | Initial office conference with Joe Blow | 1.30 200.00/hr | 260.00 |
| 04/29/94 | Telephone conference with Joe Blow Palm Springs B & S, Inc. ADF | 0.40 200.00/hr | 80.00 |
| 06/08/94 | Draft correspondence to John Kneejerk Palm Springs B & S, Inc. | 1.40 200.00/hr | 280.00 |
| 06/09/94 | Review first draft of correspondence to John Kneejerk initial revisions Palm Springs B & S, Inc. and ADF | 0.40 200.00/hr | 80.00 |
| 06/10/94 | Telephone conference with Joe Blow Palm Springs B & S, Inc. and ADF | 0.20 200.00/hr | 40.00 |

195

| | | | |
|---|---|---|---|
| 06/10/94 | Dictate revisions to correspon-<br>dence to John Kneejerk<br>Palm Springs B & S, Inc. and<br>ADF | 0.50<br>200.00/hr | 100.00 |
| 06/12/94 | Review and finalize draft of<br>correspondence to John Knee-<br>jerk; miscellaneous telephone<br>conference with Joe Blow; dic-<br>tate service instructions for<br>Monday morning to home and<br>office<br>Palm Springs B & S, Inc. and<br>ADF | 1.20<br>200.00/hr | 240.00 |
| 06/13/94 | Telephone conference with Joe<br>Blow<br>Palm Springs B & S, Inc. and<br>ADF | 0.20<br>200.00/hr | 40.00 |
| | Telephone conference with Diana<br>Macbeen at office to set ap-<br>pointment for 6/29/94 meeting<br>to review annual figures with<br>Joe Blow, Diana Macbeen, Gary<br>Deck, and Keith Barla<br>Palm Springs B & S, Inc. and<br>ADF | 0.30<br>200.00/hr | 60.00 |
| 06/15/94 | Telephone conference with Joe<br>Blow<br>Palm Springs B & S, Inc. ADF | 0.20<br>200.00/hr | 40.00 |
| 06/29/94 | Office conference with Joe<br>Blow; attend meeting at ac-<br>countants' office for year end<br>bonus discussion with John<br>Kneejerk<br>Palm Springs B & S, Inc. and<br>ADF | 1.30<br>200.00/hr | 260.00 |
| | Total Fees and Costs: | 7.90 | $1,580.00 |
| | Additional charges: | | |
| 05/05/94 | Cost Advanced: Obtain copy of<br>order of distribution for Es-<br>tate of Blow<br>Palm Springs B & S, Inc. and<br>ADF | | 15.00 |

| | | |
|---|---|---:|
| 05/09/94 | COSTS ADVANCED: Datasearch, Inc. for corporate search of records<br>Palm Springs B & S, Inc. and ADF | 52.50 |
| 06/13/94 | Cost Advanced: Hand delivery by process server of correspondence to home and office of John Kneejerk @ $21.00 ea.<br>Palm Springs B & S, Inc. and ADF | 42.00 |

|  |  |
|---|---:|
| Total Costs: | $109.50 |
| Total amount of this bill: | $1,689.50 |
| 04/14/94 Payment—thank you | ($1,000.00) |
| Balance due within ten days: | $689.50 |

# APPENDIX D

# Petition for Probate

<table>
<tr><td colspan="2">ATTORNEY OR PARTY WITHOUT ATTORNEY (NAME AND ADDRESS):    TELEPHONE NO.:</td><td>FOR COURT USE ONLY</td></tr>
<tr><td colspan="2">ATTORNEY FOR (NAME):</td><td></td></tr>
</table>

SUPERIOR COURT OF CALIFORNIA, COUNTY OF

STREET ADDRESS:

MAILING ADDRESS:

CITY AND ZIP CODE:

BRANCH NAME:

ESTATE OF (NAME):

Decedent

**PETITION FOR**

☐ PROBATE OF WILL AND FOR LETTERS TESTAMENTARY
☐ PROBATE OF WILL AND FOR LETTERS OF ADMINISTRATION WITH WILL ANNEXED
☐ LETTERS OF ADMINISTRATION
☐ SPECIAL LETTERS OF ADMINISTRATION
☐ AUTHORIZATION TO ADMINISTER UNDER THE INDEPENDENT ADMINISTRATION OF ESTATES ACT

CASE NUMBER:

HEARING DATE:

DEPT.:    TIME:

1. Attorney requests publication in (name of newspaper):

_____    _____
(Type or print name)          (Signature of attorney)

2. Petitioner* (name of each):

   requests that

   a. ☐ decedent's will and codicils, if any, be admitted to probate.

   b. ☐ (name):

       be appointed (1) ☐ executor        (3) ☐ administrator
                 (2) ☐ administrator with will annexed    (4) ☐ special administrator
       and Letters issue upon qualification.

   c. ☐ authority be granted to administer under the Independent Administration of Estates Act.

   d. ☐ bond not be required for the reasons stated in attachment 2d.

       ☐ bond be fixed at $ _____ to be furnished by an authorized surety company or as otherwise provided by law *(specify reasons if the amount is different from the minimum required by section 541 of the Probate Code)*

       ☐ deposits at *(specify institution)*:
       in the amount of $ _____ be allowed. Receipts will be filed.

3. a. Decedent died on (date):        at (place):

       ☐ a resident of the county named above.

       ☐ a non-resident of California and left an estate in the county named above located at *(specify location permitting publication in the newspaper named in item 1)*:

   b. Street address, city, and county of decedent's residence at time of death:

   c. Character and estimated value of the property of the estate

       Personal property:    $ _____
       Annual gross income from
           ☐ real property    $ _____
           ☐ personal property    $ _____
                  Total:    $ _____
       Real property:  $ _____

   d. ☐ Will waives bond.

       ☐ All beneficiaries have waived bond and the will does not require a bond *(affix waiver as attachment 3d)*.

       ☐ All heirs at law have waived bond *(affix waiver as attachment 3d)*.

   e. ☐ Decedent died intestate.

       ☐ Copy of decedent's will dated:        ☐ and codicil dated:
       is affixed as attachment 3e.

<table>
<tr><td>Form Approved by the<br>Judicial Council of California<br>Revised Effective January 1, 1981<br>DE-110(81)</td><td>(Continued on reverse)<br><br>PETITION FOR PROBATE</td><td>*All petitioners must sign the petition.<br>Only one need sign the declaration.</td></tr>
</table>

| ESTATE OF (NAME): | CASE NUMBER |
|---|---|
| Decedent | |

## PETITION FOR PROBATE

f. Appointment of personal representative

  (1) Appointment of executor or administrator with will annexed

  ☐ Proposed executor is named as executor in the will.

  ☐ No executor is named in the will.

  ☐ Proposed personal representative is a nominee *(affix nomination as attachment 3f(1))*.

  ☐ Other named executors will not act because of ☐ death ☐ declination ☐ other reasons *(specify in attachment 3f(1))*.

  (2) Appointment of administrator

  ☐ Petitioner is a nominee *(affix nomination as attachment 3f(2))*.

  ☐ Petitioner is related to the decedent as:

  (3) ☐ Appointment of special administrator requested *(specify grounds and requested powers in attachment 3f(3))*.

g. Proposed personal representative is a ☐ resident of California ☐ non-resident of California ☐ resident of the United States ☐ non-resident of the United States.

4. a. *(Complete in all cases.)* The decedent is survived by

  (1) ☐ spouse  ☐ no spouse

  (2) ☐ parent  ☐ no parent

  (3) ☐ child  ☐ no child

  (4) ☐ issue of predeceased child ☐ no issue of predeceased child.

b. No surviving child or issue of a predeceased child has been omitted from the list of heirs (item 6).

c. *(Complete only if no spouse or issue survived the decedent.)* The decedent

  (1) ☐ had no predeceased spouse.

  (2) ☐ had a predeceased spouse whose heirs are named in the list of heirs (item 6).

  (3) ☐ had a predeceased spouse who had no heirs.

d. *(Complete only if no parent or issue survived the decedent.)* The decedent is survived by

  (1) ☐ a brother or sister or issue of a predeceased brother or sister. None has been omitted from the list of heirs (item 6).

  (2) ☐ no brother or sister or issue of a predeceased brother or sister.

5. ☐ Decedent's will does not preclude independent administration of this estate under sections 591-591.7 of the Probate Code.

6. The names, residence or mailing addresses, relationships, and ages of heirs, devisees, predeceased devisees, legatees, and predeceased legatees so far as known to petitioner are ☐ listed below ☐ listed in attachment 6.

| NAME AND RELATIONSHIP | AGE | RESIDENCE OR MAILING ADDRESS |
|---|---|---|

7. ☐ Number of pages attached:

Dated: . . . . . . . . . . . . . . . . . . .

_____
(Signature of petitioner)

I declare under penalty of perjury under the laws of the State of California that the foregoing is true and correct and that this declaration is executed on (date): . . . . . . . . . . . at (place) . . . . . . . . . . . . . . .

. . . . . . . . . . . . . . . . . . .
(Type or print name)

_____
(Signature of petitioner)

# APPENDIX E

# Insurance Company Settlement Offer Agreement

## CERTIFICATE OF GOOD FAITH

XYZ Insurance Company makes the following representations to you, the claimant (or claimants), to induce you to enter into a binding agreement in order to fully and finally settle all claims for damages arising out of that certain incident that occurred on the _____ day of _____, 19____ at the following location _____ wherein you are asserting a claim for damages against our insured _____.

1. That _____, whose signature will be affixed to this document, is a duly authorized representative of XYZ Insurance Company and has the authority to sign this agreement.

2. XYZ Insurance Company is making you a good faith offer of $_____ for a full, complete and final offer to settle and compromise your claim in its entirety.

   The term "Good Faith", as used in this document includes but is not limited to the following: (A) your claim has been evaluated by senior officials of XYZ Insurance Company, taking into consideration the police report, if any, all investigative materials that the Company has gathered, all information and data provided by you, medical reports provided by you together with all costs of medical care, treatment, medications and the nature and extent of your injuries whether temporary, permanent or partially permanent, the results of an independent examination, if any; (B) the degree of fault or negligence of both your and our insured; (C) the amount of settlement judge, arbitrator and jury awards in comparable cases; (D) other factors such as your age, employment history, loss of wages and/or earning power, and (E) other pertinent matters.

3. It is the opinion of XYZ Insurance Company that the offer made is reasonable in consideration of all circumstances and it is the highest offer of settlement this Company will make, based upon the facts presented.

4. This document and the release of liability which is being presented for you to sign is an offer of compromise and settlement only and cannot be used in evidence in any court of law in the event you do not accept our offer.

5. If at a later date you feel that XYZ Insurance Company has not acted in good faith you may sue this Company and this document may be entered into evidence. If you sue and are unsuccessful you agree to pay our attorneys fees and costs. If you are successful in such a lawsuit for bad faith XYZ Insurance Company will pay your reasonable and necessary fees and costs.

200

Page 2

6.   You, the claimant, represent by signing this agreement that you have disclosed any and all facts within your knowledge, including but not limited to your present medical condition and all other information concerning future medical problems together with any other information you have that might be beneficial to your claim.

7.   XYZ Insurance Company recognizes that you are relying on this Certificate of Good Faith in entering into the proposed settlement.


Dated _____ at _____ _____
                                      XYZ Insurance Company


Dated _____ at _____ _____
                                      Claimant



STATE OF _____

COUNTY OF _____

On _____, before me _____, personally appeared _____
_____, personally known to me OR proved to me on the basis of satisfactory evidence to be the person whose name is subscribed to the within instrument and acknowledged to me that he executed the same in his authorized capacity, and that by his signature on the instrument the person, or the entity upon behalf of which the person acted, executed the instrument.

WITNESS my hand and official seal.


_____
Signature of Notary Public

# APPENDIX F

# Petition for Marriage Dissolution

| ATTORNEY OR PARTY WITHOUT ATTORNEY *(Name and Mailing Address)*: | TELEPHONE NO.: | FOR COURT USE ONLY |
|---|---|---|
| ATTORNEY FOR *(Name)*: | | |

SUPERIOR COURT OF CALIFORNIA, COUNTY OF

STREET ADDRESS:

MAILING ADDRESS:

CITY AND ZIP CODE:

BRANCH NAME:

MARRIAGE OF

  PETITIONER:

  RESPONDENT:

| | CASE NUMBER: |
|---|---|

**PETITION FOR**

☐ **Dissolution of Marriage**  ☐ **And Declaration Under Uniform**
☐ **Legal Separation**            **Child Custody Jurisdiction Act**
☐ **Nullity of Marriage**

1. RESIDENCE (Dissolution only) ☐ Petitioner ☐ Respondent has been a resident of this state for at least six months and of this county for at least three months immediately preceding the filing of this Petition for Dissolution of Marriage.

2. STATISTICAL FACTS
   a. Date of marriage:
   b. Date of separation:
   c. Period between marriage and separation
      Years:        Months:

3. DECLARATION REGARDING MINOR CHILDREN OF THIS MARRIAGE FOR WHOM SUPPORT MAY BE ORDERED OR WHO MAY BE SUBJECT TO CUSTODY OR VISITATION ORDERS
   a. ☐ There are no minor children.     b. ☐ The minor children are:
      Child's name          Birthdate          Age     Sex

   c. IF THERE ARE MINOR CHILDREN, COMPLETE EITHER (1) OR (2)
      (1) ☐ Each child named in 3b is currently living with ☐ petitioner ☐ respondent
         in the following county *(specify)*:
         During the last five years each child has lived in no state other than California and with no person other than petitioner or respondent or both. Petitioner has not participated in any capacity in any litigation or proceeding in any state concerning custody of any minor child of this marriage. Petitioner has no information of any pending custody proceeding or of any person not a party to this proceeding who has physical custody or claims to have custody or visitation rights concerning any minor child of this marriage.
      (2) ☐ A completed Declaration Under Uniform Child Custody Jurisdiction Act is attached.

4. ☐ Petitioner requests confirmation as separate assets and obligations the items listed
   ☐ in Attachment 4  ☐ below:
      Item                                                   Confirm to

> NOTICE: Any party required to pay child support must pay interest on overdue amounts at the "legal" rate, which is currently 10 percent. This can be a large added amount.

(Continued on reverse)

Form Adopted by Rule 1281
Judicial Council of California
1281 (Rev. January 1, 1995)

PETITION
(Family Law)

Family Code, §§ 2330, 3409
Calif. Rules of Court, rule 1215

| MARRIAGE OF *(last name, first name of parties)*: | CASE NUMBER: |
|---|---|
| | |

**5. DECLARATION REGARDING COMMUNITY AND QUASI-COMMUNITY ASSETS AND OBLIGATIONS AS CURRENTLY KNOWN**
- a. ☐ There are no such assets or obligations subject to disposition by the court in this proceeding.
- b. ☐ All such assets and obligations have been disposed of by written agreement.
- c. ☐ All such assets and obligations are listed ☐ in Attachment 5 ☐ below *(specify)*:

**6. Petitioner requests**
- a. ☐ Dissolution of the marriage based on
  - (1) ☐ irreconcilable differences. FC 2310(a)
  - (2) ☐ incurable insanity. FC 2310(b)
- b. ☐ Legal separation of the parties based on
  - (1) ☐ irreconcilable differences. FC 2310(a)
  - (2) ☐ incurable insanity. FC 2310(b)
- c. ☐ Nullity of void marriage based on
  - (1) ☐ incestuous marriage. FC 2200
  - (2) ☐ bigamous marriage. FC 2201
- d. ☐ Nullity of voidable marriage based on
  - (1) ☐ petitioner's age at time of marriage. FC 2210(a)
  - (2) ☐ prior existing marriage. FC 2210(b)
  - (3) ☐ unsound mind. FC 2210(c)
  - (4) ☐ fraud. FC 2210(d)
  - (5) ☐ force. FC 2210(e)
  - (6) ☐ physical incapacity. FC 2210(f)

**7. Petitioner requests that the court grant the above relief and make injunctive (including restraining) and other orders as follows:**

|  | Petitioner | Respondent | Joint | Other |
|---|---|---|---|---|
| a. Legal custody of children to | ☐ | ☐ | ☐ | ☐ |
| b. Physical custody of children to | ☐ | ☐ | ☐ | ☐ |
| c. Child visitation be granted to | ☐ | ☐ | ☐ | ☐ |
| ☐ supervised as to *(specify)*: | | | | |
| d. Spousal support payable by (wage assignment will be issued) | ☐ | ☐ | | |
| e. Attorney fees and costs payable by | | | | |

- f. ☐ Terminate the court's jurisdiction (ability) to award spousal support to respondent.
- g. ☐ Property rights be determined.
- h. ☐ Wife's former name be restored *(specify)*:
- i. ☐ Other *(specify)*:

**8.** If there are minor children of this marriage, the court will make orders for the support of the children without further notice to either party. A wage assignment will be issued.

**9.** I have read the restraining orders on the back of the Summons, and I understand that they apply to me when this petition is filed.

I declare under penalty of perjury under the laws of the State of California that the foregoing is true and correct.

Date:

▶ _____
(SIGNATURE OF PETITIONER)

.......... (TYPE OR PRINT NAME OF ATTORNEY) ..........

▶ _____
(SIGNATURE OF ATTORNEY FOR PETITIONER)

**NOTICE:** Please review your will, insurance policies, retirement benefit plans, credit cards, other credit accounts and credit reports, and other matters you may want to change in view of the dissolution or annulment of your marriage, or your legal separation. However, some changes may require the agreement of your spouse or a court order (see Family Code sections 231–235).

## APPENDIX G

# Response to Petition for Dissolution

| ATTORNEY OR PARTY WITHOUT ATTORNEY *(Name and Mailing Address)*: | TELEPHONE NO.: | FOR COURT USE ONLY |
|---|---|---|
| | | |

ATTORNEY FOR *(Name)*:

**SUPERIOR COURT OF CALIFORNIA, COUNTY OF**

STREET ADDRESS:

MAILING ADDRESS:

CITY AND ZIP CODE:

BRANCH NAME:

**MARRIAGE OF**

PETITIONER:

RESPONDENT:

| | CASE NUMBER: |
|---|---|

**RESPONSE** ☐ **and REQUEST FOR**

☐ Dissolution of Marriage     ☐ **And Declaration Under Uniform**
☐ Legal Separation                   **Child Custody Jurisdiction Act**
☐ Nullity of Marriage

1. **RESIDENCE** (Dissolution only) ☐ Petitioner ☐ Respondent has been a resident of this state for at least six months and of this county for at least three months immediately preceding the filing of this Petition for Dissolution of Marriage.

2. **STATISTICAL FACTS**
   a. Date of marriage:                 c. Period between marriage and separation
   b. Date of separation:              Years:        Months:

3. **DECLARATION REGARDING MINOR CHILDREN OF THIS MARRIAGE**
   a. ☐ There are no minor children.      b. ☐ The minor children are:

   | Child's name | Birthdate | Age | Sex |
   |---|---|---|---|
   | | | | |

   c. IF THERE ARE MINOR CHILDREN, COMPLETE EITHER (1) OR (2)
   (1) ☐ Each child named in 3b is currently living with ☐ petitioner ☐ respondent
   in the following county *(specify)*:
   and during the last five years has lived in no state other than California and with no person other than petitioner or respondent or both. Respondent has not participated in any capacity in any litigation or proceeding in any state concerning custody of any minor child of this marriage. Respondent has no information of any pending custody proceeding or of any person not a party to this proceeding who has physical custody or claims to have custody or visitation rights concerning any minor child of this marriage.
   (2) ☐ A completed Declaration Under Uniform Custody of Minors Act is attached.

4. ☐ Respondent requests confirmation as separate assets and obligations the items listed
   ☐ in Attachment 4 ☐ below:
   Item                                       Confirm to

---

**NOTICE:** Any party required to pay child support must pay interest on overdue amounts at the "legal" rate, which is currently 10 percent. This can be a large added amount.

---

(Continued on reverse)

Form Adopted by Rule 1282
Judicial Council of California
1282 [Rev. January 1, 1995]

**RESPONSE**
(Family Law)

Family Code, § 2020
Calif. Rules of Court, rule 1215

| MARRIAGE OF *(last name, first name of parties)*: | CASE NUMBER: |
|---|---|

5. DECLARATION REGARDING COMMUNITY AND QUASI-COMMUNITY ASSETS AND OBLIGATIONS AS CURRENTLY KNOWN
   - a. ☐ There are no such assets or obligations subject to disposition by the court in this proceeding.
   - b. ☐ All such assets and obligations have been disposed of by written agreement.
   - c. ☐ All such assets and obligations are listed ☐ in Attachment 5 ☐ below:

6. ☐ Respondent contends there is a reasonable possibility of reconciliation.

7. ☐ Respondent denies the grounds set forth in item 6 of the petition.

8. ☐ Respondent requests
   - a. ☐ Dissolution of the marriage based on
     - (1) ☐ irreconcilable differences. FC 2310(a)
     - (2) ☐ incurable insanity. FC 2310(b)
   - b. ☐ Legal separation of the parties based on
     - (1) ☐ irreconcilable differences. FC 2310(a)
     - (2) ☐ incurable insanity. FC 2310(b)
   - c. ☐ Nullity of void marriage based on
     - (1) ☐ incestuous marriage. FC 2200
     - (2) ☐ bigamous marriage. FC 2201
   - d. ☐ Nullity of voidable marriage based on
     - (1) ☐ respondent's age at time of marriage FC 2210(a)
     - (2) ☐ prior existing marriage. FC 2210(b)
     - (3) ☐ unsound mind. FC 2210(c)
     - (4) ☐ fraud. FC 2210(d)
     - (5) ☐ force. FC 2210(e)
     - (6) ☐ physical incapacity. FC 2210(f)

9. Respondent requests the court grant the above relief and make injunctive (including restraining) and other orders as follows:

|  | Petitioner | Respondent | Joint | Other |
|---|---|---|---|---|
| a. Legal custody of children to .......................................... | ☐ | ☐ | ☐ | ☐ |
| b. Physical custody of children to ....................................... | ☐ | ☐ | ☐ | ☐ |
| c. Child visitation be granted to ........................................ | ☐ | ☐ | ☐ | ☐ |
| ☐ supervised as to *(specify)*: | | | | |
| d. Spousal support payable by (wage assignment will be issued) ................ | ☐ | ☐ | | |
| e. Attorney fees and costs payable by ................................... | ☐ | ☐ | | |

f. ☐ Terminate the court's jurisdiction (ability) to award spousal support to petitioner.
g. ☐ Property rights be determined.
h. ☐ Wife's former name be restored *(specify)*:
i. ☐ Other *(specify)*:

10. If there are minor children of this marriage, the court will make orders for the support of the children without further notice to either party. A wage assignment order will be issued.

I declare under penalty of perjury under the laws of the State of California that the foregoing is true and correct.

Date:

▶ _____
(SIGNATURE OF RESPONDENT)

▶ _____
(TYPE OR PRINT NAME OF ATTORNEY)      (SIGNATURE OF ATTORNEY FOR RESPONDENT)

| The original response must be filed in the court with proof of service of a copy on petitioner. |
|---|

RESPONSE
(Family Law)

# Schedule of Assets for Dissolution

| ATTORNEY OR PARTY WITHOUT ATTORNEY *(Name and Address)*: | TELEPHONE NO. |
|---|---|
| | |

ATTORNEY FOR *(Name)*:

SUPERIOR COURT OF CALIFORNIA, COUNTY OF RIVERSIDE

MARRIAGE OF
PETITIONER:

RESPONDENT:

| SCHEDULE OF ASSETS AND DEBTS ☐ Petitioner's ☐ Respondent's | CASE NUMBER |
|---|---|

## — INSTRUCTIONS —

List all your known community and separate assets or debts. Include assets even if they are in the possession of another person, including your spouse. If you contend an asset or debt is separate, put H or W in the first column (separate property) to indicate to whom you contend it belongs.

All values should be as of the date of signing the declaration unless you specify a different valuation date with the description.

For additional space, use a continuation sheet numbered to show what item is being continued.

| ITEM NO. | ASSETS—DESCRIPTION | SEP. PROP. | DATE ACQUIRED | CURRENT GROSS FAIR MARKET VALUE | AMOUNT OF MONEY OWED OR ENCUMBRANCE |
|---|---|---|---|---|---|
| | | | | $ | $ |
| 1. | REAL ESTATE *(Give street addresses and attach copies of deeds with legal descriptions and latest lender's statement.)* | | | | |
| 2. | HOUSEHOLD FURNITURE, FURNISHINGS, APPLIANCES *(Identify)* | | | | |
| 3. | JEWELRY, ANTIQUES, ART, COIN COLLECTIONS, etc. *(Identify)* | | | | |

(Continued on reverse)

Page one of four

Form Approved by Rule 1292.11
Judicial Council of California
1292.11 (New July 1, 1990)

Form 479.11

**SCHEDULE OF ASSETS AND DEBTS**
**(Family Law)**

Code of Civil Procedure. §§ 2030(c). 2033.5

| ITEM NO. | ASSETS — DESCRIPTION | SEP. PROP. | DATE ACQUIRED | CURRENT GROSS FAIR MARKET VALUE | AMOUNT OF MONEY OWED OR ENCUMBRANCE |
|---|---|---|---|---|---|
| 4. | VEHICLES, BOATS, TRAILERS *(Describe and attach copy of title document.)* | | | $ | $ |
| 5. | SAVINGS ACCOUNTS *(Account name, account number, bank, and branch. Attach copy of latest statement.)* | | | | |
| 6. | CHECKING ACCOUNTS *(Account name and number, bank, and branch. Attach copy of latest statement.)* | | | | |
| 7. | CREDIT UNION, OTHER DEPOSIT ACCOUNTS *(Account name and number, bank, and branch. Attach copy of latest statement.)* | | | | |
| 8. | CASH *(Give location.)* | | | | |
| 9. | TAX REFUND | | | | |
| 10. | LIFE INSURANCE WITH CASH SURRENDER OR LOAN VALUE *(Attach copy of declaration page for each policy.)* | | | | |

(Continued on next page)

Appendix H

| . ITEM NO. | ASSETS—DESCRIPTION | SEP. PROP. | DATE ACQUIRED | CURRENT GROSS FAIR MARKET VALUE | AMOUNT OF MONEY OWED OR ENCUMBRANCE |
|---|---|---|---|---|---|
| | | | | $ | $ |
| 11. | STOCKS, BONDS, SECURED NOTES, MUTUAL FUNDS *(Give certificate number and attach copy of the certificate or copy of latest statement.)* | | | | |
| 12. | RETIREMENT AND PENSIONS *(Attach copy of latest summary plan documents and latest benefit statement.)* | | | | |
| 13. | PROFIT-SHARING, ANNUITIES, IRAS, DEFERRED COMPENSATION *(Attach copy of latest statement.)* | | | | |
| 14. | ACCOUNTS RECEIVABLE AND UNSECURED NOTES *(Attach copy of each.)* | | | | |
| 15. | PARTNERSHIPS AND OTHER BUSINESS INTERESTS *(Attach copy of most current K–1 form and schedule C.)* | | | | |
| 16. | OTHER ASSETS | | | | |
| 17. | TOTAL ASSETS FROM CONTINUATION SHEET | | | | |
| 18. | TOTAL ASSETS | | | $ | $ |

(Continued on reverse)

1292.11 [New July 1, 1990]
Form 479.11

**SCHEDULE OF ASSETS AND DEBTS**
(Family Law)

| ITEM NO. | DEBTS—SHOW TO WHOM OWED | SEP. PROP. | TOTAL OWING | DATE INCURRED |
|---|---|---|---|---|
| 19. | STUDENT LOANS *(Give details.)* | | $ | |
| 20. | TAXES *(Give details.)* | | | |
| 21. | SUPPORT ARREARAGES *(Attach copies of orders and statements.)* | | | |
| 22. | LOANS—UNSECURED *(Give bank name and loan No. and attach copy of latest statement.)* | | | |
| 23. | CREDIT CARDS *(Give creditor's name and address and the account number. Attach copy of latest statement.)* | | | |
| 24. | OTHER DEBTS *(specify)*: | | | |
| 25. | TOTAL DEBTS FROM CONTINUATION SHEET | | | |
| 26. | TOTAL DEBTS | | $ | |

27. ☐ _____ pages are attached as continuation sheets.

I declare under penalty of perjury under the laws of the State of California that the foregoing is true and correct.

Date:

. . . . . . . . . . . . . . . . . . . . . . . . . . . . . . . . . . . . . . . . .
(TYPE OR PRINT NAME OF DECLARANT)                    (SIGNATURE OF DECLARANT)

1292.11 [New July 1, 1990]                    **SCHEDULE OF ASSETS AND DEBTS**                    Page four of four
Form 479.11                                        (Family Law)

# Bibliography

Beck, Susan and Orey, Michael, "Skaddenomics: The Ludicrous World of Law Firm Billing," *American Lawyer*, Sept. 1991, pp. 91–97.

Carbonara, Peter, "I'm From Missouri. Show Me," *American Lawyer*, July/August, 1990, pp. 34–38.

Desoff, Alan and Cleesatte, "Hanging by a Thread," *National Jurist*, Oct/Nov, 1992, pp. 14–21.

Dolan, Maura, "When the Lawyer's Bill Is Out of Bounds," L.A. *Times*, July 16, 1994, pp. A1, A21.

Galen, Michele, Cuneo, Alice, and Greising, David, "Guilty," *Business Week*, April 13, 1992, pp. 60–66.

Glendon, Mary Anne, *A Nation Under Lawyers*, New York: Farrar, Straus & Giroux, 1994.

Gordon, James D. "Secrets of the Bar," *Orange County Lawyer*, April, 1992, p. 12–15.

Griffin, Alice, *Personal Bankruptcy*, New York: Cakewalk Press, 1993.

Linowitz, Sol with Mayer, Martin, *The Betrayed Profession*, New York: Scribners & Sons, 1994.

McCormack, Mark H., *The Terrible Truth About Lawyers*, New York: Beech Tree Books, 1987.

Marston, David, *Malice Aforethought*, New York: William Morrow, 1991.

Rachlin, Jill, *Kiplinger's Handbook of Personal Law*, Washington, D.C.: Kiplinger Books, 1995.

Raitt, G. Emmett, Jr., "What If Your Client Used Value Billing?" *Orange County Lawyer*, April 1992, pp. 37–39.

Warner, Ralph, *The Independent Paralegal's Handbook*, Berkeley: Nolo Press, 1993.

"Those #*X!! Lawyers," *Time*, April 10, 1978, pp. 56–59.

# Index

ABA. *See* American Bar
  Association
Academy of Family Mediators, 150
Account administrators (credit
  managers), 20–21
Adjectives test for overlawyering,
  82–83
Administrator of estate, 161,
  168–70
Adoptions, 54
Adversarial frame of mind, 6–10
Advertising, xv, xvi, xviii, 101
  bankruptcy and, 115–16
  lawyer pools and, 60
  personal injury and, 135, 137,
    141–42
"Affidavit of Service" form, 95–96
Alcohol abuse of lawyers, 89–90
Aleshire, David, 7–8, 101
Alimony
  bankruptcy and, 107, 110
  death and, 160
  divorce and, 146, 151, 154, 155
Alpha Publications, 112
American Arbitration Association
  (AAA), 53
American Bar Association (ABA),
  xii, 32, 35

Model Rules of, 97–98
National Discipline Data Bank
  of, 97
American Express, 58
American Pre-Paid Legal Services
  Institute, 59
American Trial Lawyers
  Association (ATLA), xv–xvi.
  *See also* Consumer Lawyers
  of America
"Am Law 100" survey, 30–31
Arbitration
  as alternative to lawyers, 52–53
  divorce and, 149–50
  fee, 85–86
  personal injury and, 140–41
Arizona, 154–55
ATLA. *See* American Trial
  Lawyers Association
Attitude checklist, 185–86
Attitude problems, 90
Attorneys. *See* Lawyers; *and
  specific topics*
Attorneys' Referral Services, 57
Attorney Theory of Relativity,
  25–26
Auditing firms, 84–85
Automatic stay, 108

Axiom of Delayed Rewards, 13

Bailey, F. Lee, 7
Bala Cynwyd, 84
Bankruptcy, xviii, 54, 105–18, 137
  billing practices and, 14, 64
  do-it-yourself, 111–13
  reasons to declare, 107–9
  selection of lawyers for, 113–18
  types of, 109–11
Bankruptcy chasers, 114–15
Bankruptcy Code, 107, 115
Bar associations. *See also*
    American Bar Association
  filing complaints with, 97–100
  referrals of, 57
Baron, David, 102
Beck, Susan, 36
Belli, Melvin, 121–22
*Beyond the Billable Hour: An
    Anthology of Alternative
    Billing Methods* (ABA), 35
Big Guns, 123
Bill, sample, 195–97
Billing practices, xii–xiv, xviii, 12,
    14–48, 64, 74
  cap on fees and, 72, 168
  contingency fee, 14–15, 64, 65,
    94, 96, 137–39
  contracts and, 77
  cost minimization and, 71–74
  criminal law and, 131–32
  estimated cost and, 65, 72
  fax machines and, 28–29
  flat fee, 14, 64
  by the hour, xiv, 15, 30–31, 64,
    137–39, 168
  monthly, 72–73
  novice indoctrination process
    and, 16–19
  overcharging and, 15–24, 101
    client complaints, 20–21
  personal injury and, 137–39
  photocopy machines and, 27–28,
    31
  probate and, 166–71
    appeal of fees, 170–71

stalling and, 37–48
  depositions, 45–47
  discovery rule, 42–44
  interrogatories, 44–45
  mandatory settlement
    conferences (MSCs), 47–48
  writs and motions, 39–42
  telephone calls and, 17–20, 48,
    76
  car phones, 29
  travel and, 25–27
  value billing and, 33–35, 74
  warning signs, 90
    fee renegotiation, 92–93
Bond indentures, 22–24
Bradley Trusts, 27
Buddy system, 169

California, 59, 181
  divorce in, 154–55
  lawyers in, xi–xii
  paralegals in, 54
  personal injury suits in, 79
  probate in, 165, 166
  wills in, 164
California State Bar, xvii
Capping operations, 143–44
Car accidents, personal injury
    and, 138–39
Car phones, 29
Case law, 8–9
Cases. *See also* Lawsuits
  definition of, 8
  reviewing of, 18
Chapman and Cutler, 21
Chapter 7 bankruptcy, 105,
    109–10, 112, 113, 115–18
Chapter 11 bankruptcy, 106, 108,
    110–11
Chapter 13 bankruptcy, 110, 112,
    113, 115, 117–18
Child support
  bankruptcy and, 107, 110
  divorce and, 146, 151, 154, 155,
    157
Citicorp, 27–30
Civil rights, xvi